Black Americans in World War II

Black Americans in World War II

A. Russell Buchanan

Clio Books

Santa Barbara, California   Oxford, England

Library of Congress Cataloging in Publication Data

Buchanan, Albert Russell, 1906–
  Black Americans in World War II.

  Bibliography: p.
  Includes index.
  1. World War, 1939–1945—Afro-Americans.
  2. United States—Race question. I. Title.
  D810.N4B82   940.54'03   76-53577
  ISBN 0-87436-277-6

American Bibliographical Center—Clio Press
2040 Alameda Padre Serra
Santa Barbara, California 93103

European Bibliographical Center—Clio Press
Woodside House, Hinksey Hill
Oxford OX15 BE, England

First paperback printing January 1979
Paperbound ISBN 0-87436-290-3

Manufactured in the United States of America

To Ethel

Acknowledgments

I should like to thank the editors of the Clio Press, Dr. Eric H. Boehm and Mr. Lloyd W. Garrison, for inclusion of this work in the publications of their press, and especially Mr. Garrison for his careful editorial counsel. Thanks go also to Paulette Wamego for her scrupulous performance as copy editor. I am grateful to officials of the Manuscript Division of the Library of Congress for making it possible for me to study the files of the National Urban League and the National Association for the Advancement of Colored People. Acknowledgment should also go to the Committee on Research of the Academic Senate of the University of California, Santa Barbara, for financial assistance and to numerous librarians in the University Library of the University of California for many courtesies. Mr. James McCarthy provided useful research assistance in the early phases of my research. As always, I owe a debt, which cannot be expressed adequately here, to my wife, Ethel, for unfailing support and encouragement.

Contents

CHAPTER 1

1940

BLACK AMERICANS especially felt the impact of World War II. They served in the armed forces and played various roles on the home front, either working in war plants, maintaining homes, or attending school under wartime conditions. They also continued their struggle to attain equality of status with other Americans. This narrative summarizes the progress made by Negroes[1] during the course of World War II.

It is useful here to establish a point of reference by briefly examining the status of Negroes in 1940, when Europe was at war and the United States was headed for involvement. At that time there were 12,865,518 Negro Americans, 9.8 percent of the entire population of the United States. Of these, 9,904,619 were in the South; 2,790,193 were in the North; and 170,706 in the West.[2] The existence, side by side, of two races created a dilemma in the South. The Civil War ended the enslavement of Negroes by whites, but the whites continued to dominate the Negroes after Reconstruction. Whites determined relationships between the two peoples and established the rules of behavior. Most whites maintained that the only way for the two races to exist satisfactorily together was for both to understand clearly and irrevocably that whites were superior and Negroes inferior. Whites ensured this state of affairs through segregation, which was effected by a social code of "etiquette." The code was observed by whites and Negroes in their daily relationships, and it continually reminded Negroes of their perpetually inferior status. In the South, customs and traditions, even more than laws, sanctioned the preservation of this etiquette, and actually resorting to law tended to indicate a weakening of the customs and traditions.[3] The thesis of white

---

[1] The word "Negro" is used in this study, since it was generally used at the time. There are numerous discussions of this matter. For example, see Roi Ottley, *Inside Black America* (London: Eyre & Spottiswoode, 1948), pp. 215–17.

[2] U.S. Office of Education, *National Survey of the Higher Education of Negroes*, vol. 4, *A Summary*, by Ambrose Caliver (Washington, D.C.: U.S. Government Printing Office, 1943), p. 2.

[3] The many works on this subject include: John Dollard, *Caste and Class in a Southern Town* (New Haven: Yale University Press, 1937); Charles S. Johnson, *Patterns of Negro Segregation* (New York: Harper & Brothers, 1943); Hortense Powdermaker, *After Freedom: A Cultural History of the Deep South* (New York: Viking Press, 1939); Allison Davis, Burleigh B. Gardner,

supremacy supported by the idea that southern whites knew best
what was good for the Negro and for the South created strong
resentment against interference by northerners or the federal
government.

By 1940, rifts appeared in the traditional image of life in the
South. There were few overt threats to the establishment, no mas-
sive shift from nonaggression to aggression, no widespread break-
down of segregation, and no general abandonment of the social
rules which kept it functioning. Certain factors, however, produced cracks which at the time appeared to be minor flaws in the
system but which led to major breaks following World War II.

The development of the privately owned automobile brought
Negroes fresh annoyances and major benefits. Negroes who owned
cars could avoid the "Jim Crow" restrictions they encountered on
public transportation. Although efforts were initially made to preserve segregation, automobile transportation simply did not lend
itself to those efforts. It was impossible to create a dual network
of roads, one for whites, another for Negroes; so all drivers, regardless of color, had to observe common rules of the road. White
drivers, for instance, could not insist on the right-of-way over
Negro drivers, since it was not feasible to check identities at in-
tersections. Negroes, however, learned to drive with care, since
they could expect that blame would be more readily placed on
them in the event they were involved in accidents.[4]

Service stations helped break down the rules of segregation,
since they could not provide separate pumps for white and Negro
customers, and few provided separate restrooms. Needs of Negroes
were initially ignored, but service station facilities were gradually
opened to all. The problems of eating and sleeping while traveling
remained, and some Negro motorists were unable to find accommodations. A motorist green-book appeared, to assist Negro travel-
ers in finding places to eat and sleep without embarrassment.[5] The
movement of Negroes from one region in the South to another
created a new problem for segregationists, since Negroes soon dis-
covered that the codes of etiquette they were expected to observe
were not uniform.[6]

---

and Mary R. Gardner, *Deep South* (Chicago: University of Chicago Press,
1941); Bertram Wilbur Doyle, *The Etiquette of Race Relations in the South:
A Study in Social Control* (1937; Port Washington, N.Y.: Kennikat Press,
1968).

[4] Powdermaker, *After Freedom*, p. 49.

[5] Maurice R. Davie, *Negroes in American Society* (New York: Whittlesey
House, 1949), pp. 296–97.

[6] Doyle, *Etiquette*, p. 148.

The growth of southern cities also mitigated the effects of seg-regation and social etiquette. Impersonal rules for masses of Ne-groes remained; Negroes were barred from restaurants, hotels, and stores, and they had restricted access to streetcars, theaters, and places of recreation. However, face-to-face encounters between whites and Negroes on busy city sidewalks were hardly conducive to the subservience whites had come to expect from Negroes. The anonymity of the metropolis permitted Negroes to go their own ways, unless they had personal or business dealings with whites. The fear of what the white man might do correspondingly dimin-ished.[7]

Negroes began to drift from rural areas to southern cities and also to move to the North. The 1940 census showed 47.9 percent of southern Negroes lived in urban areas, 35.2 percent on rural farms, and 16.8 percent in rural nonfarm areas.[8] This shift indi-cated that despite poor educational opportunities more Negroes were getting better educations. The radio and movies gave young Negroes a glimpse of what they were missing and of what the American dream might be. They began to see that the southern code was not cast in concrete. Life in large cities enabled many Negroes to become independent, largely separate, from whites. They began to enter the professions and establish their own stores, schools, and better living quarters. Upper- and middle-class Ne-groes thus often avoided contact with whites and lower-class Ne-groes.[9]

In the North, a few Negroes of northern ancestry since colonial times were first slaves and then became free.[10] Later, the Negro population was increased by escaped slaves from the antebellum South, who managed to stop short of Canada. These groups, aug-mented by a trickle from the border states after the war, developed a kind of class system. The upper crust was well educated and some were professionals who made a living from their fellow Ne-

---

[7] Allison Davis and John Dollard, *Children of Bondage: The Personality Development of Negro Youth in the Urban South* (Washington, D.C.: Ameri-can Council on Education, 1940), p. 201.

[8] Charles S. Johnson, "The Negro Minority," *Annals of the American Academy of Political and Social Science* 223 (September 1942): 12.

[9] For example, see Robert L. Sutherland, *Color, Class, and Personality* (Washington, D.C.: American Council on Education, 1942), p. 23.

[10] For summary accounts of pre–World War I Negroes in the North, see E. Franklin Frazier, *The Negro in the United States*, rev. ed. (New York: Macmillan, 1957), pp. 242–72; Robert C. Weaver, *The Negro Ghetto* (New York: Harcourt, Brace, 1948), p. 23; Gunnar Myrdal, *An American Dilemma: The Negro Problem and Modern Democracy* (New York: Harper & Row, 1962), pp. 183–201.

groes and who were respected by members of both races. Most northern Negroes, however, were servants and unskilled workers. The First World War produced an influx of southern Negroes attracted by job opportunities in northern war plants.[11] As Negroes poured into Detroit and Chicago, they met with serious problems in adjusting from rural to urban life.[12] An urban Negro middle class also developed, comprised of Negro businessmen and professionals who helped serve the greatly expanded Negro urban population.[13] Middle-class Negroes took advantage of their educational opportunities to move into a status similar to that of the white middle class, but they still lacked equality. The educated, intelligent, and sensitive Negro knew full well the extent of the gap that remained.

In 1940, young Negroes who were born in or who had grown up in the North knew nothing firsthand of the segregation practiced in the South and were unfamiliar with its daily reminder of inferiority. They lived in a kind of residential segregation peculiar to the North and were acquainted with other aspects of racism. Their parents told them about the gap between the races that still existed, or they experienced it themselves. Nevertheless, compared to Negroes in the rural South, northern Negroes had made great progress toward equality.

Two important organizations, the National Urban League and the National Association for the Advancement of Colored People, represented Negro interests. The National Urban League, founded in 1907, began as an interracial organization and, during the interwar period, depended heavily on the financial support of the white community. The league's main office in New York City maintained branch offices in forty-six cities. In retrospect, the National Urban League developed leaders in its national and branch offices who dealt effectively with middle- and upper-class whites and gained the general respect of both races. The league was interested in practical, everyday matters and was not concerned with

11 See Louise Venable Kennedy, *The Negro Peasant Turns Cityward* (1930; New York: AMS Press, 1968), pp. 52–54.

12 See Chicago Commission on Race Relations, *The Negro in Chicago: A Study of Race Relations and a Race Riot* (Chicago: University of Chicago Press, 1922), pp. 106–40; St. Clair Drake and Horace R. Cayton, *Black Metropolis: A Study of Negro Life in a Northern City* (New York: Harcourt, Brace, 1945), pp. 58–64.

13 Myrdal, *American Dilemma*, pp. 309–10, 316–17. See also Abram L. Harris, *The Negro as Capitalist: A Study of Banking and Business Among American Negroes* (1936; College Park, Md.: McGrath, 1968).

the development of broad social objectives, at least not if that involved neglect of specific issues. The league cast its lot with the employer class; so it was conspicuously unsuccessful in dealing with workers at large and in organized labor. The effectiveness of the league at that time cannot be entirely discounted because as Gunnar Myrdal stated, "Negroes and Whites in America deal with each other through the medium of plenipotentiaries."[14] The Urban League trained men and women to speak to whites in language they understood, without subservience.

The National Association for the Advancement of Colored People was more prominent than the Urban League, but its beginnings were similar in that it was interracial and received white financial support. The NAACP started as a result of a protest, the shock shared by whites and Negroes over a race riot which occurred in, of all places, Abraham Lincoln's hometown, Springfield, Illinois. The NAACP was also headquartered in New York City and maintained branch offices throughout the nation. The NAACP management was interracial. The president was white, but the dominant official during World War II, Walter White, the secretary, was a Negro, as were all members of the New York staff. Like the National Urban League, the NAACP was primarily successful in its dealings with the middle and upper classes. The NAACP differed in that it worked for specific objectives, such as the reversal of a court case, and openly enunciated the long-range goal of complete equality for Negroes. The NAACP program in 1940 included demands for:[15]

1. Antilynching legislation.
2. Legislation to end peonage and debt slavery among the sharecroppers and tenant farmers of the South.
3. Enfranchisement of the Negro in the South.
4. Abolition of injustices in legal procedure, particularly criminal procedure, based solely upon color or race.
5. Equitable distribution of funds for public education.
6. Abolition of segregation, discrimination, insult, and humiliation based on race or color.

---

[14] Myrdal, *American Dilemma*, p. 724. The National Urban League held to the ideal of interracial effort during the war. In a speech to the annual conference of the National Urban League, September 28, 1943, Lester B. Granger asserted: "Perhaps the greatest service which the League has rendered during these periods has been its unwavering demonstration of the fact that interracial cooperation does exist throughout America, and can work." In NAACP Files, 1943 (270:3).

[15] Cited in Myrdal, *American Dilemma*, p. 820.

7. Equality of opportunity to work in all fields with equal pay for equal work.
8. Abolition of discrimination against Negroes in the right to collective bargaining through membership in organized labor unions.

The basic doctrine of the NAACP remained interracial, but by 1936, Negroes assumed effective control over its formulation. The NAACP was important to the Negro leadership. Walter White developed to a high degree the art of "access" to influential whites, in and out of the government, and he became a hard-hitting leader in difficult racial situations. The organization also provided a livelihood, sometimes precarious because of a lack of funds, for young Negroes, who also gained valuable experience. The NAACP developed in an era which produced highly successful pressure groups, and it adopted strategies and tactics in common with them.[16] The organization, for instance, operated under centralized control. The Washington bureau performed a variety of key tasks: analyzing bills before Congress, maintaining voting records, relaying this information to local offices, and contacting government leaders. The Washington staff frequently appeared before congressional committees and other governmental bodies. A national publication of the NAACP, *Crisis*, was an important means of disseminating information and ideas.

As a pressure group, the NAACP brought its influence to bear in four areas. From the outset it attempted to arouse the public's awareness of the Negro struggle toward political and civil rights. The public relations department used all of the available media. The NAACP made little headway in the South, and its southern offices encountered strong opposition from those whites who viewed the association as a radical organization. In the legislative field, the association focused on specific issues rather than on an effort to establish a Negro political bloc. The Washington bureau helped pressure legislators when such issues as Jim Crow, lynching, or poll tax legislation were being considered. The NAACP also exerted pressure on members of the administration, and a prime case in point was its support in 1940 of the projected March on Washington. Another important activity was designed to further Negro rights through the courts. In this regard the NAACP approach was conservative, since the association's attor-

---

[16] For a careful study of the NAACP as a pressure group, see Warren D. St. James, *The National Association for the Advancement of Colored People: A Case Study in Pressure Groups* (New York: Exposition Press, 1958).

neys normally sought favorable decisions on specific cases rather than confronting the courts with more fundamental issues.

Organized labor provided another very important training ground for the Negro leadership. Negroes originally placed in minor or token roles gained experience and the confidence of their fellow white workers. More and more Negroes were selected on merit, rather than on the basis of their color, especially at the local level. The all-Negro unions also helped Negroes develop leadership qualities because heads of these groups gained experience in working with the members of their own organizations and in dealing with leaders of other labor unions and the representatives of industry. For example, the Brotherhood of Sleeping Car Porters was led by one of the ablest and most articulate Negro leaders of his day, A. Philip Randolph. As a result of Randolph's efforts, the National Mediation Board gave the brotherhood sole jurisdiction over the railroad porters in 1935, and in 1936 the American Federation of Labor gave the brotherhood a national charter. Randolph continued his fight against racial discrimination within the AFL. Negro labor leaders frequently associated themselves with the Negro "improvement and protest" organizations and thus developed other opportunities for leadership. Negro leaders in business and industry often differed with labor leaders or at least were apathetic toward what they were attempting to do.

Other prominent Negroes (Myrdal labeled them "glamour personalities") performed a valuable service for the Negro people. Prior to World War II some Negroes became distinguished performers in the arts and sports and were more widely known than almost any other Negroes. Although they generally avoided public leadership, Negro athletes and artists raised Negro self-esteem. The accomplishments of Joe Louis in boxing, Paul Robeson in football and music, Eddie Tolan in track, Willis Ward and Kenny Washington in football, Roland Hayes and Marian Anderson in music, and many others evoked racial pride of Negroes throughout the nation.

In summary, Negro leadership, on the eve of the entry of the United States into World War II, possessed its greatest potential in the North because there was a wider range of activity there than in the South. Negro radicals and their white counterparts made little headway, although Negro leaders in the North were more activist in the sense that they could protest more openly and demand status as well as welfare objectives. The ensuing war extended these opportunities in some ways and restricted them in others. Negro leaders learned tactics and procedures, and the NAACP and the National Urban League provided them on-the-job training. They learned the techniques of pressure groups and published their own journals. In addition to the National Urban League's *Opportunity* and the NAACP's *Crisis,* there were about 150 Negro-run weekly newspapers in the United States. Some metropolitan newspapers ran twenty to twenty-five pages and generally were comprised of about 70 percent news, 25 percent features, and 5 percent editorials. They tended to supplement the regular newspapers by providing news of interest to Negroes which other papers lacked. Negro newspapers were addressed primarily to the middle and upper classes and did not reach the masses. A chain of radical papers, with Communist leanings, attempted with some success to gain the support of the lower economic groups.

The Negro press was described by a contemporary in these words: "Traditionally our press is a special pleader; it is an advocate of human rights. Its whole history is written in the blood and travail of men who spent themselves unselfishly in the cause of freedom." He noted the real problems of the Negro press and continued, "How to *advocate* our cause without suffering the prohibitions which modern business placed upon *agitation* is a question which every Negro publisher has to answer in defining a business policy that will blend with the ideals for which the Negro press must contend."[17]

The Negro of 1940 was far short of achieving the goal of full civil rights. In his volume *Federal Protection of Civil Rights,* Robert K. Carr quotes Supreme Court Justice Robert Jackson as saying that the individual in this country is protected from slavery and involuntary servitude by "both a shield and a sword." Carr elaborated by noting that the "shield" consists of a number of "constitutional guarantees of specific rights" which the court may invoke for the protection of the individual.[18] The courts were slow to give the Negro protection from encroachments by federal and state governments and provided little protection from private individuals. The "shield" provided by the Constitution, legal interpretations, and constitutional amendments proved to be inadequate, so Carr noted the need of a "sword" of "positive power by a government which looks upon interference with one man's

----

17 P. B. Young, "The Negro Press—Today and Tomorrow," *Opportunity* 17 (July 1939): 205.

18 Robert K. Carr, *Federal Protection of Civil Rights: Quest for a Sword* (Ithaca, N.Y.: Cornell University Press, 1947), pp. 3–5.

civil rights by another man as conduct that is criminal in character and should be treated accordingly."[19] Since those who needed protection were usually in a minority of some sort, state governments were slow to take up the "sword" in their behalf, particularly because of local pressures. The federal government, to which minorities looked for help, was also slow to assume this role.

Shortly before World War II, however, a federal "sword" was finally forged. Attorney General Frank Murphy created the Civil Liberties Unit within the Criminal Division of the Department of Justice on February 3, 1939. He detailed its objectives as follows:[20]

> The function and purpose of this unit will be to make a study of the provisions of the Constitution of the United States and Acts of Congress relating to civil rights with reference to present conditions, to make appropriate recommendations in respect thereto, and to direct, supervise and conduct prosecutions of violations of the provisions of the Constitution or Acts of Congress guaranteeing civil rights to individuals.

The Civil Rights Section, as it came to be called, was established because of Frank Murphy's personal interest in civil liberty and at a favorable time because of other developments. The Supreme Court was showing signs of developing a more aggressive approach toward the protection of civil rights and the Federal Bureau of Investigation, established in 1908, was developing into an effective federal police force. That development was a necessary factor in the successful prosecution of crime by federal agencies.

Congress also showed more concern about civil rights. The activities of the La Follette Civil Liberties Committee, a subcommittee of the Senate Committee on Education and Labor, gained national publicity with its mandate "to investigate violations of rights of free speech and assembly and interference with the right of labor to organize and bargain collectively."[21] The La Follette Committee existed from 1936 to 1941 and received more attention

---

19 Carr, *Federal Protection of Civil Rights,* p. 20.

20 Order of the Attorney General, No. 3204, February 3, 1939, cited in Carr, *Federal Protection of Civil Rights,* p. 24. On January 30, 1939, Walter White wrote to Attorney General Frank Murphy supporting the establishment of a separate bureau "to preserve the civil liberties of citizens." White to Murphy, January 30, 1939. In NAACP Files, 1943 (273:2).

21 S. Res. 266, 74th Cong., 2d sess., June 6, 1936.

than the Civil Rights Section, which worked slowly and quietly to clarify the Constitution and statutory laws under which it was to operate. The section found that it could clarify many points but that there were uncertainties in the law. Subsequently the section brought several cases to court to test its legal powers.

The Negro also made limited, but significant, gains in the legislation passed by many northern states. After the Supreme Court invalidated federal civil rights legislation passed during Reconstruction, the northern states began to pass their own civil rights bills. Those bills included provisions for equal accommodations in public places and the right of all citizens to serve on juries. In 1933, for example, a New York law declared that no public utility could refuse to employ a person on account of race, color, or religion.

The rights of Negroes in connection with education depended greatly on the section of the country in which they resided. In the South, segregation in the schools was maintained by state laws upheld by the Supreme Court in several notable cases, e.g., *Cumming v. Board of Education* (1899); *Berea College v. Kentucky* (1908); *Gong Lum v. Rice* (1927). Generally, the Court avoided the direct question of the constitutionality of segregation and acted on specific cases.

During the 1930s two cases involving higher education produced slight breaks in the segregation issue. One, *Pearson v. Murray* (1936), arose when the University of Maryland School of Law denied admission to a Negro solely on account of his race and offered the applicant an out-of-state scholarship to cover his education. The court did not rule on the issue of segregated education, but it found that equality for the Negro could be gained only by admitting him to a white school of law in Maryland. The more widely known case of *Missouri ex rel. Gaines v. Canada* (1938) took much the same stand. In that decision the court stated: "The basic consideration is not as to what sort of opportunities other States provide, but as to what opportunities Missouri itself furnishes to White students and denies to Negroes solely upon the ground of color." The *Gaines* doctrine, as it was called, did not result in the admission of Negroes to white professional schools in the South. Rather, it persuaded six southern states—Missouri, Texas, Florida, Louisiana, North Carolina, and South Carolina—to create separate law schools for Negroes.

The border states followed a middle course on segregation in education; they tended to make segregation optional, as in the case of Kentucky. This view extended north into Indiana, where the legislature allowed the local community the option of building separate schools when the Negro population warranted it. Other northern states, however, passed laws prohibiting segregation.[22] Nevertheless, such laws failed to guarantee desegregation, and when Negroes settled in large numbers in northern cities, school segregation developed. When Negroes lived in separate parts of a city their children tended to fill the schools in those areas, and administrative action and sometimes community pressure made segregation complete. A small minority, whites and Negroes, was reassigned to other schools.

Prior to World War II, the Negro made no gains in the right to use public transportation in the South, where the "separate but equal" doctrine established in *Plessy v. Ferguson* (1896) was the order of the day. The antidiscrimination provision of the Interstate Commerce Act of 1887 failed to change southern practices.

Segregated housing also severely restricted Negroes, although they had made limited, but disappointing, gains by 1940. Legal attempts to limit Negroes to certain residential areas were made at the local level. An ordinance passed in Baltimore, Maryland, in 1910 set a pattern followed by several southern and border cities. The Supreme Court invalidated a Louisville, Kentucky, ordinance which prohibited both Negroes and whites from living in sections of the city populated largely by people of the other color, in *Buchanan v. Warley* (1917).

The Court's decision did not stop segregation. Instead, the advocates of racial segregation shifted to another device, the restrictive covenant, i.e., an agreement of white property owners not to sell or rent to Negroes. One such covenant was tested in a District of Columbia court in 1923 and the court held that the covenant did not invade the constitutional rights of Negroes "inasmuch as they had the right to enter into agreements to keep Whites or other persons deemed undesirable out of colored neighborhoods."[23] The Supreme Court declined to review the case as being outside its jurisdiction. In the case of *Hansberry v. Lee* (1940), the Supreme Court decision appeared to be a victory for anti-

---

22 Johnson, *Patterns of Negro Segregation*, pp. 183–85.
23 Cited in Richard Sterner, *The Negro's Share: A Study of Income, Consumption, Housing and Public Assistance* (New York: Harper & Brothers, 1943), pp. 207–8.

segregationists because the Court held that no one case involving a parcel of land could be used as a precedent for other cases.[24] Actually, the trend seemingly favored more rather than less segregation, and the Federal Housing Administration contributed to this trend by giving credit to Negroes only if they wished to build or buy in Negro neighborhoods, and to whites for similar investments in white sections.[25] This government agency, therefore, made more money available to Negroes but at the cost of extending segregation of the races.

One of the areas of greatest contrast between North and South was the franchise. Northern Negroes had the vote but southern Negroes did not, at least not when their vote had any possible influence. The extralegal white primary was more important than various legal restrictions in the attempt to deny Negroes the right to vote. The return of political control to whites in the South after Reconstruction resulted in the "solid South," one political party rather than two. Regular elections, consequently, were pro forma verifications of the real races and decisions made in the Democratic primaries. By 1940, the poll tax had been dropped by three states, Florida, Louisiana, and North Carolina, but where it remained it was far less significant than the white primary in denying Negroes their right to vote.[26] The legality of the white primary was principally tested in Texas, where numerous cases led to a key decision in *United States v. Classic* (1941). The suit was initiated by the Civil Rights Section and several issues were involved, but on the issue of the white primary the court held that the power of the Congress under the Constitution included "the authority to regulate primary elections when, as in this case, they are a step in the exercise by the people of their choice of representatives in Congress." The court stressed that under the law of the state involved, the primary was "an integral part of the election machinery." The *Classic* decision set the stage for an eventual invalidation of the white primary but the definitive decision came in 1944 in *Smith v. Allwright*,[27] since the possibility of

24 See Drake and Cayton, *Black Metropolis*, pp. 186–87. The Chicago NAACP was involved in handling this case. See St. James, *The National Association for the Advancement of Colored People*, p. 240; Milton R. Konvitz, "A Nation Within a Nation: The Negro and the Supreme Court," *Opportunity* 20 (June 1942): 175.

25 Sterner, *Negro's Share*, pp. 312–16. See also Myrdal, *American Dilemma*, pp. 348–50.

26 V. O. Key, Jr., *Southern Politics in State and Nation* (New York: Alfred A. Knopf, 1949), pp. 578, 618.

27 For editorial comments, see *Monthly Summary of Events and Trends in Race Relations* 1:9 (May 1944): 24–27.

claiming that all primaries were not covered by the *Classic* decision remained.

By 1940, millions of Negroes were acquainted with the federal government, in most cases through a connection with one of the federal agencies created during the New Deal. In general, Negroes learned that they could expect more from the federal government than from local governments. Negro leaders became experienced in the use of pressure tactics to deal with farm and labor issues. Representatives of the NAACP and the National Urban League lobbied hard in Washington and became well known to federal officials from the president down.[28]

By 1940, Negroes were employed in larger numbers by the federal government and this important connection became increasingly significant during the war years. Following the setback suffered during the Wilson administration, the number of Negro employees rose during the 1920s, especially in the postal service.[29] The Census Bureau was desegregated and so were some of the offices in the Department of Commerce.

The percentage of Negroes in the prewar administration of President Franklin D. Roosevelt rose slightly over that of the 1920s, and it is important to note that there was an increase in openings at higher levels.[30] The gains were, at best, only a start. In 1938, 90 percent of the Negroes employed by the government were in the custodial services, 10 percent were scattered in other categories.[31] On November 7, 1940, the Ramspeck Act on Civil Service banned discrimination in employment on account of color, race, or religious beliefs.

Two important developments took place at the upper level of employment. First, several Negroes were hired as special assistants to Cabinet members to deal with matters affecting Negroes. For example, Robert C. Weaver and William H. Hastie were employed by the Department of the Interior, and one of the nation's

---

28 See Raymond Wolters, *Negroes and the Great Depression: The Problem of Economic Recovery* (Westport, Conn.: Greenwood, 1970), pp. 39–51.

29 Sterling D. Spero and Abram L. Harris, *The Black Worker: The Negro and the Labor Movement* (1931; Port Washington, N.Y.: Kennikat Press, 1966), p. 122.

30 Samuel Krislov, *The Negro in Federal Employment: The Quest for Equal Opportunity* (Minneapolis: University of Minnesota Press, 1967), pp. 22–23.

31 Gladys M. Kammerer, *Impact of War on Federal Personnel Administration 1939–1945* (Lexington: University of Kentucky Press, 1951), p. 53. For example, in the Federal Works Agency (as of May 1940) 3132 of 3442 Negro workers were listed as custodial workers. See W. J. Trent, Racial Relations Officer, Federal Works Agency, to Lester B. Granger, October 11, 1940. In National Urban League Files, Series VI, Box 13.

leading Negro women, Mary McLeod Bethune, took leave from the presidency of Bethune-Cookman College in Florida to become director of the Division of Negro Affairs of the National Youth Administration (NYA).[32] It was largely at Bethune's instigation that a new "Black Cabinet" came into being. The informal group, composed of a shifting number of prominent Negroes in Washington, was called together and presided over by Bethune. Her friendship with President Roosevelt enabled her to take many of the ideas of the group directly to him.[33] Second, the practice of calling prominent Negroes to Washington as consultants on special occasions or for particular purposes was revived. Presidents Theodore Roosevelt and William Howard Taft consulted with Booker T. Washington from time to time, and President Franklin D. Roosevelt expanded the practice during World War II.

---

[32] Rackham Holt, *Mary McLeod Bethune: A Biography* (Garden City, N.Y.: Doubleday, 1964), pp. 191–92.

[33] See Mary McLeod Bethune, "My Secret Talks with FDR," *Ebony* (April 1949): 42–51.

CHAPTER 2

Prototype 1941:
March on Washington

NEGROES IN THE UNITED STATES lived with rising hopes and, at the same time, increasing frustrations during the prewar months. The hopes were a blend of patriotic and racial impulses, and, as it became evident that the United States would become a belligerent, Negroes sought to be of service to their country. Negroes believed they should be able to participate fully in the war effort, either as members of the armed forces or by producing weapons of war. Obstacles of one sort or another diminished those expectations, and frustration became widespread. The issue came to a climax with the announced March on Washington scheduled for July 1, 1941.[1] The episode is worth studying as part of an examination of the Negro leadership because conservatives became activists and a few radicals remained aloof from what was purported to be a great mass movement.

The proposed march envisaged the participation of thousands of Negroes, but it was originated by one man and carried out by relatively few people. Negroes were increasingly annoyed because restrictions were imposed on young men who wished to join the armed services and because of the injustices they met when they did. Barriers to wartime employment also increased Negro resentment. Negro leadership sought to change the situation. The Negro press publicized the issues and repeatedly described incidents involving discrimination and prejudice. Negro leaders pressured Washington officials. On September 27, 1940, President Roosevelt, Secretary of the Navy Frank Knox, and Assistant Secretary of War Robert P. Patterson met with A. Philip Randolph, Walter White, and T. Arnold Hill (formerly industrial secretary of the National Urban League) to confer on the utilization of Negro manpower in the army.[2] The result was not what the Negro participants anticipated.

---

[1] For a detailed account of the march, see Herbert Garfinkel, *When Negroes March: The March on Washington Movement in the Organizational Politics for FEPC* (Glencoe, Ill.: Free Press, 1959).

[2] Garfinkel, *When Negroes March*, p. 34.

The conference initially gave the Negro leaders a slight reason for optimism. The Selective Service and Training Act was approved on September 16, 1940, and the War Department issued a press release entitled "Expansion of Colored Organizations Planned." The release stated that 36,000 of the first 400,000 men to be drafted would be Negroes, and it listed several Negro units, including those established in August 1940. The release mentioned the Civil Aeronautics Administration and thus implied that Negro air corps units would be established. The release suggested there would be gains for the Negro, and the Negro leaders went to the conference with additional requests. They presented a seven-point memorandum which stressed the need for fuller participation by and integration of Negroes in all units of the armed forces. They recommended that officers already commissioned and those to be trained serve in "all branches of the service" including all activities in aviation, not merely as pilots. Existing units of the army should "accept and select officers and enlisted personnel without regard to race."[3]

The relationship of the War Department to the Negro will be considered in detail later; but as part of the background on the March on Washington, it is sufficient here to note that as a result of the meeting of September 27, a memorandum prepared by Assistant Secretary of War Patterson, approved informally by the secretary and by the president, was issued to the press. The first part of the statement encouragingly announced that the War Department's policies toward the services of Negroes would be on a "fair and equitable basis." The strength of Negro personnel in the army would be comparable to the Negro proportion of the total population. The rest of the memorandum, however, made it clear that "the policy of the War Department is not to intermingle colored and white enlisted personnel in the same regimental organizations." Regular units were "going concerns," and "no experiments should be tried with the organizational setup of these units at these critical times." The document stated without further explanation: "Negroes are being given aviation training as pilots, mechanics, and technical specialists. This training will be accelerated."[4]

The resulting disappointment with the memorandum was in-

---

3 Ulysses Lee, *The Employment of Negro Troops*, The United States Army in World War II: Special Studies (Washington, D.C.: U.S. Government Printing Office, 1966), pp. 74–75.
4 Cited in Lee, *Employment of Negro Troops*, pp. 75–76.

tensified when it was implied during the press conference that the document was supported by Negro leaders who had met with President Roosevelt. White, Hill, and Randolph issued a hotly worded statement which denied their complicity and asserted that "official approval by the Commander-in-Chief of the Army and Navy of such discrimination and segregation is a stab in the back of democracy."[5] Under the pressure of a presidential campaign, the administration repudiated the statement that the three Negro leaders had agreed to the War Department announcement. The War Department did not change the statement; nevertheless, the administration made other efforts to assuage the feelings of Negroes. Most important, William H. Hastie, dean of Howard University School of Law, was appointed as Secretary of War Stimson's civilian aide on Negro affairs. On the same day another Negro, Colonel Benjamin O. Davis, was nominated for promotion to brigadier general, and the appointment was later confirmed.[6]

The attention of Negro leaders turned toward war production, a problem which will be considered in some detail in Chapter 3. The National Urban League had long been concerned with Negro employment. At the local level, its forty-six branches gathered information on the subject and attempted to promote the training and employment of Negroes. Leaders in the national organization concluded that something needed to be done at the national level to counter the resistance and apathy of American businessmen toward involving the Negro in war production. The NAACP leadership reached a similar conclusion, and leaders of both groups approached various agencies of the federal government, especially the new National Defense Advisory Council. Fortunately, Sidney Hillman, head of the council's Division of Labor Training and Supply, had appointed Robert C. Weaver as his assistant. Weaver was instrumental in having a clause against racial discrimination inserted in the council's instructions to employers. The clause, however, proved to be without force.[7]

Negro leaders and the Negro press were especially incensed because the aircraft industry refused to hire Negroes except in menial capacities. The National Urban League also found that boards of education and other agencies discouraged and hindered

---

[5] Walter White, *A Man Called White: The Autobiography of Walter White* (New York: Viking Press, 1948), p. 187.

[6] Lee, *Employment of Negro Troops*, p. 79.

[7] Lester B. Granger, "The President, the Negro, and Defense," *Opportunity* 19 (July 1941): 205.

Negroes from enrolling in training courses on the ground that their efforts would be wasted, since jobs were not open to them in the aircraft industry.

The press campaign revealed a strong popular interest on the part of Negroes throughout the country. Some 6,000 Negroes, for example, assembled in the municipal auditorium in Kansas City in a protest sponsored by the National Urban League.[8] In November 1940, Negro and white leaders met at Hampton Institute in Virginia in the conference on Participation of the Negro in National Defense. The recommendations made during the conference apparently carried little weight, and some Negroes were led to think that more than words would be needed to solve the problem.

A. Philip Randolph had been giving serious thought to the issue of the Negro and the war. In January 1941 he called a meeting in Washington of several prominent Negroes, including Walter White, Mary McLeod Bethune, Dr. Channing H. Tobias (senior secretary of the National Council of the YMCA), Dr. George E. Haynes (executive secretary of the Federal Council of Churches of Christ), and Lester B. Granger (executive secretary of the National Urban League). Randolph then recommended that the Negro people march on Washington "to exact their rights in National Defense employment and the armed forces of the country."[9]

On March 26, 1941, Randolph called for another meeting to be held in New York on the third of April. He wrote that he had been thinking about the discrimination facing Negroes in their search for jobs in war production and concluded "that the use of the method of mass pressure should be given serious consideration by Negroes in their fight for their rights as American citizens."[10] He, therefore, called on a group of representatives to consider plans for a march on Washington. During the meeting a small committee, including Randolph, White, and, later, Granger, was organized to plan the proposed march.[11] Randolph then went south to organize local committees in Richmond and

---

[8] Louis Ruchames, *Race, Jobs, & Politics: The Story of FEPC* (New York: Columbia University Press, 1953), pp. 13–14.

[9] Garfinkel, *When Negroes March*, p. 196 n.

[10] A. Philip Randolph to Lester B. Granger, March 26, 1941. In National Urban League Files, Series VI, Box 11.

[11] Randolph to Granger, April 7, 1941; Granger to Dr. Rayford W. Logan, April 14, 1941. In National Urban League Files, Series VI, Box 11.

Atlanta and plan additional committees in other southern cities.[12] He expected the sale of dollar certificates and buttons to help finance the program.

At the outset, reaction to the proposal for a march on Washington was low-keyed. One newspaper reported that if only 2,000 Negroes marched on Washington "that would be an accomplishment of considerable import."[13] The proposed march needed support from a major figure and Randolph's stature among Negroes gave the proposal weight. It is significant that with one or two exceptions the Negro press both backed and publicized his proposed march. The attitude of the leaders of the National Urban League and the NAACP is more difficult to diagnose. White and Granger clearly gave the march their personal support, as did the directors of the NAACP. Curiously, however, the NAACP continued planning an annual convention to meet from June 24 to 29 in Houston, a considerable distance from Washington. The march was scheduled for July 1, and Randolph was scheduled to speak at the NAACP convention—billed as head of his union and not as chairman of the March on Washington Committee. Even more unusual, neither the National Urban League's *Opportunity* nor the NAACP's *Crisis,* both official media, mentioned the forthcoming march until it was called off.[14]

It appears that the leaders of these two important Negro organizations were willing to support the march personally without publicly committing their organizations to a march on Washington. It must be remembered that the National Urban League and even the NAACP favored traditional methods of achieving their goals, such as lobbying in Washington and testing the laws in the courts. The proposed advance of thousands of Negroes on the capital while the world was at war was a different matter. The leaders of local chapters of organizations like the National Urban League naturally sought the guidance of their headquarters as to what stance to take.[15] On May 20, 1941, Lester B. Granger wrote a memorandum to the executive secretaries of local branches:[16]

---

[12] Randolph (from Atlanta) to Granger, May 6, 1941. In National Urban League Files, Series VI, Box 11.

[13] *Pittsburgh Courier,* February 8, 1941.

[14] See Garfinkel, *When Negroes March,* pp. 38–42.

[15] E. Maurice Moss, Executive Secretary, National Urban League, Pittsburgh, to Granger, May 14, 1941; May 22, 1941. In National Urban League Files, Series VI, Box 11.

[16] Granger Memo to Executive Secretaries, May 20, 1941. In National Urban League Files, Series VI, Box 11.

I have joined Mr. Randolph as a cosponsor of the official call, but I have done this as an individual and not representing the organization. . . . Organizations are not represented as such in the sponsoring committee, since it is desired to avoid organizational rivalry and jealousies and to make this a mass demonstration of the attitude of Negro citizens.

A week earlier Granger wrote the industrial secretary of the New Orleans branch and predicted that Randolph would "arouse enough enthusiasm to produce a pretty good attendance, even if it comes from the Washington area." On the other hand, he did not believe that "any as far from Washington as the New Orleans branch should go out on a limb encouraging people to go at too great an expense."[17] Granger and others were clearly wary of setting up a new organization that might duplicate or rival the work of existing groups, since a campaign in the journals of these two bodies could bring into the open a cleavage of Negro opinion on the tactics to be followed. The number of persons said to be ready to march on Washington rose from 10,000 to 100,000, while the actual preparation of people planning to go to Washington remained conveniently vague.

Granger later termed the proposed March on Washington a "gigantic gamble."[18] No one, even the leaders, apparently knew how many would participate but the uncertainty did not disturb them. The Negroes decided, significantly, to "go it alone," and only Negroes were invited to participate in the march. Herbert Garfinkel noted that one purpose of the decision was to rule out participation by Communists. Randolph left the National Negro Congress when Communists gained control, and he was determined to keep them out of the March on Washington. Negro Communists by themselves were not sufficiently numerous or strong to cause trouble, and the Communist party in America wavered in its attitude toward the proposed march.[19]

During May the press campaign widely publicized the March on Washington Committee's call for people to join the march. The call outlined the objectives: "To this end we propose that

---

17 Granger to Clarence A. Laws, Industrial Secretary, National Urban League, New Orleans, May 15, 1941. In National Urban League Files, Series VI, Box 11.

18 Granger, "The President," p. 204.

19 Garfinkel, *When Negroes March,* pp. 42–53; Wilson Record, *The Negro and the Communist Party* (Chapel Hill: University of North Carolina Press, 1951), pp. 202–6.

ten thousand Negroes MARCH ON WASHINGTON FOR JOBS IN NA-
TIONAL DEFENSE AND EQUAL INTEGRATION IN THE FIGHTING FORCES
OF THE UNITED STATES."[20] In the ensuing campaign, the press first
ballooned the figure to 50,000 and then to 100,000.

People who gamble can never be sure of the outcome, and official Washington began to react as the date set for the march
neared. Members of the administration wrote to Negro leaders
asking them to call it off. White liberals who had supported the
Negroes but opposed a march on the nation's capital were deeply
disturbed. Eleanor Roosevelt wrote to Randolph on June 10, to
indicate that she had discussed the matter with the president and
urged Randolph to cancel the march. She argued that the timing
was wrong, that crusades were "valuable and necessary sometimes," but not "when the temper is as tense as it is at present."[21]

Mrs. Roosevelt arranged to meet a few days later in Mayor
Fiorello La Guardia's office in the New York City Hall with the
mayor, Aubrey Williams (administrator of the National Youth
Administration), Walter White, and A. Philip Randolph. Mrs.
Roosevelt restated her fear that the march would increase the
opposition of southern congressmen and others unsympathetic to
Negroes. La Guardia, who was chairman of the Office of Civilian
Defense, and Williams joined the effort to dissuade Randolph
from continuing his plans, but he was adamant, saying: "The
march must go on. I am certain it will do some good. In fact, it
has already done some good; for if you were not concerned about
it you wouldn't be here now discussing the question of racial
discrimination."[22]

On June 14, the New York committee of the March on Washington met to discuss the meeting called by Mrs. Roosevelt. Randolph, the chairman, described the views of Mrs. Roosevelt and
Mayor La Guardia, their opposition to the proposed march, and
their agreement that something ought to be done for Negroes
immediately. According to the minutes of the meeting, Walter

---

20 The statement also declared: "In this period of power politics, nothing
counts but pressure, more pressure, and still more pressure, through the
tactic and strategy of broad, organized, aggressive mass action behind the vital
and important issues of the Negro." The statement, however, sternly coun-
seled "against violence and ill-considered and intemperate action and the
abuse of power." Copy of statement from Negroes' Committee to March on
Washington for Equal Participation in National Defense to March July 1,
1941. In National Urban League Files, Series VI, Box 11.

21 Cited in Ruchames, *Race, Jobs, & Politics,* p. 17.

22 Earl Brown, "American Negroes and the War," *Harper's Magazine* (April
1942): 549.

White added that Mrs. Roosevelt suggested that White and Randolph confer with the president and Stimson, Knox, Hillman, La Guardia, William Knudsen (co-director, Office of Production Management), and Jesse Jones (Secretary of Commerce). White recommended that three demands be presented at the meeting:

1. Forbid giving government contracts to concerns that practice racial discrimination. Those plants that persist in the practice should be taken over by the government, and order maintained there by the army, as in the case of the recent strike controversy.
2. Abolish segregation in the army.
3. Abolish segregation in all departments of the government in Washington.

Granger took the most conservative point of view in the discussion that followed, but the tone of the meeting was expressed by Randolph. He said that the march should not be called off unless the president issued an executive order at the time of the conference.[23]

A week later Randolph and White were called to the White House. There they met the president, the secretaries of war and the navy, Knudsen and Hillman (co-directors, Office of Production Management), Williams, and La Guardia. The meeting began with President Roosevelt's statement that he opposed the march. Randolph replied that the march would go ahead as scheduled and continued by saying that he would be willing to cancel the march if Roosevelt issued an executive order "with teeth in it." Roosevelt replied that he would not make a statement until a study of discrimination was made and a recommendation presented to him. He then asked those present to adjourn to the cabinet room to study the matter and report to him. Of course such a hastily conceived meeting could produce few results, and Secretary Stimson, the chairman, noted that time was needed to deal with the problem. He argued that progress was being made and cited the promotion of Colonel Benjamin O. Davis to brigadier general.[24]

A few days before the scheduled march, Randolph was again called to Washington, this time to meet with La Guardia and Williams. Despite La Guardia's argument that there would be

---

23 Minutes of Local Meeting of Negro March-on-Washington Committee, New York, June 14, 1941. In National Urban League Files, Series VI, Box 11.
24 Brown, "American Negroes and the War," pp. 549–50; White, *A Man Called White*, pp. 190–93.

strong southern objections to an executive order, Randolph remained firm; La Guardia then showed Randolph a tentative draft of an executive order. Randolph objected because the draft failed to include government departments as well as industry in its prohibition of discrimination on the basis of race, religion, or national origins. After debating the issue, the participants called the White House, and President Roosevelt agreed to include government departments. Randolph had gained his point, and he called off the march.

The threatened March on Washington was used by Negro leaders, notably A. Philip Randolph, to win a distinct victory. President Roosevelt issued Executive Order 8802 on June 25, 1941, and according to one expert, it "constituted the most important effort in the history of this country to eliminate discrimination in employment by use of governmental authority." Roosevelt's order created the Committee on Fair Employment Practice (FEPC) within the Office of Production Management "to receive and investigate complaints of discrimination in violation of the provisions of this order" and "to take appropriate steps to redress grievances which it finds to be valid."[25] Negroes praised the announcement as a step in the right direction and in general reacted favorably toward the first appointments to the committee, headed by Mark Ethridge, a well-known white liberal and publisher of the *Louisville Courier-Journal*.

The move by Randolph, White, and a few other Negro leaders was a gamble. There is no evidence to indicate that they would have canceled the march had they failed to obtain their objective in advance, and it is not known how many Negroes would have marched. A few Negro leaders evidently made a key decision concerning the minimum basis on which they would call off the march, specifically an executive order against discrimination in industry and government departments. The decision fell short of the initial demand for the elimination of discrimination in the armed forces, and that request disappeared without further mention during the negotiations.

In conclusion, the Negro leaders realistically made the march a weapon to be used at the conference table without actually bringing it into play. They succeeded in obtaining an executive order against discrimination in industry at a time when white labor supplies were becoming inadequate to meet the needs of

25 Franklin D. Roosevelt, *Public Papers and Addresses of Franklin D. Roosevelt* (New York: Random House, 1950), 10: 233–35.

war production. That goal was more realistic than trying to force an immediate change on the armed forces, which were bound by years of tradition—that advance would come later. Randolph, White, and their associates appeared radical in planning a mass march on Washington, but they had moderate expectations.

The threatened march and the president's FEPC order were more important to Negroes than to the rest of the country. The order was a one-day news item. The *New York Herald Tribune* gave it full front-page coverage, and the *New York Times* gave it full back-page coverage. Numerous editorials commended the president's action and just as many newspapers, including the Hearst press, ignored it. It is possible that the Negro leaders realized that the nation was not stirred by the prospect of a march on Washington and thus tempered their demands.

Following his victory, Randolph rather unrealistically tried to keep the threat of a march alive. He announced early in July that his aim was "to broaden and strengthen" March on Washington committees throughout the nation "to serve as watchdogs on the application of the President's executive order to determine how industries are complying with it."[26]

Negro support of the victory and of the decision not to march was widespread, but some who had anticipated taking part in the move on Washington felt let down by the decision. One group in New York, the Youth Division of the Negro March Committee, wrote Randolph to protest: "The March heightened the ambitions and pent-up emotions of the Negro masses as never before in the life of Negro youth." Calling the president's executive order "only a partial victory, which was not even handled as any kind of a victory," the youth committee declared that calling off the march was too high a price to pay and criticized the Negro leaders for canceling the march without "consulting the Negro masses through their local committees." The committee then recommended that no additional action be taken without consultation and that the march proceed within ninety days after the first of July. Randolph's lengthy reply compared the march to a strike and explained that the objective had been gained without resorting to the march.[27]

---

26 As quoted in Garfinkel, *When Negroes March,* p. 63. In a letter to Lester B. Granger, Randolph wrote: "We still need the Committees to function by way of watching and checking the observance of the Executive Order by the industries." Letter dated July 25, 1941. In National Urban League Files, Series VI, Box 11.

27 Letter, Youth Committee to National Executive Committee for March on Washington. Meeting of the youth committee held June 28, 1941; letter

Other leaders, Walter White and Lester B. Granger, were less enthusiastic about perpetuating the March on Washington committees, since they might rival the NAACP and the National Urban League or divide the efforts of Negroes. Randolph's reputation, however, precluded their overt opposition to his move. Further, the leaders were criticized for being satisfied with their gains and not increasing their demands; their opposition to the continuation of the March on Washington committees might well have been attacked as a lack of aggressive leadership.[28] Randolph was a member of the board of directors of the NAACP, but he was not closely associated with its destiny; so he continued to use the March on Washington committees to retain visibility as a political leader and a dominant labor figure.

After Pearl Harbor the threatened March on Washington became a less potent weapon—it would be viewed quite differently when the nation was at war. The restrictions on travel in wartime alone made the proposed march a logistical problem of considerable magnitude. In summary, Randolph continued to use the March on Washington committees as protest groups, but the threatened use of the March on Washington ceased to be a viable possibility.

Randolph had the right to attempt to keep the march movement alive because he was its originator and his union was its principal financial supporter. The March on Washington Committee as of August 5, 1941, was reported to have $2,992.26— $900.00 came from the sale of buttons, and the largest single contribution, $957.89, was made by the Brotherhood of Sleeping Car Porters. The NAACP furnished $543.00.[29] The National Urban League contributed nothing, although Granger had made the staffs of the local branches available to provide stenographic and other assistance.

---

received July 14, 1941. In National Urban League Files, Series VI, Box 11. On August 13, 1941, the March on Washington Committee, New York, issued a press release by Randolph: "Why and How the March Was Postponed." Randolph wrote: "Simply stated, the March was postponed because its main objective, namely, the issuance of an Executive Order banning discrimination in National Defense, was secured in conference with the President." The other objectives, getting Negroes into the armed forces and into all departments of the government, he stated, would be "the next step in the fight for the Negro March-on-Washington movement." In National Urban League Files, Series VI, Box 11.

28 Garfinkel, *When Negroes March*, pp. 70–71.

29 Financial Report, n.d. (as of August 5, 1941). In National Urban League Files, Series VI, Box 11. See also NAACP Board of Directors Minutes, June 26, 1941. In NAACP Files, Series A, Box 11.

Randolph was responsible for staging mass meetings in various cities during 1942, including New York in June and Detroit in September. In Detroit, Randolph announced that there would be a national conference "for the integration and expression of the collective mind and will of the Negro people."[30] The NAACP became more disenchanted, and in April 1942 its board of directors voted to contribute a sum not to exceed $250.00 to the March on Washington Committee.[31] In September the board reexamined and explained its position in a written statement which summarized the early support of the March on Washington and continued, "But the March on Washington project now proposes to set itself up as a membership body which in its announced eight-point program duplicates existing organizations."[32] The NAACP then indicated that it would not divert its energies toward any other organization. Lester B. Granger's problem was simpler, since he had never permitted the National Urban League to become formally associated with the March on Washington. Pleading the pressure of business, he resigned from the March on Washington Committee in September 1942.[33]

Randolph was undeterred by the declining support and proceeded to plan for a national conference. Roy Wilkins, of the NAACP, attended and reported to Walter White on the conference, which took place in Chicago, June 30 to July 4, 1943. His tone was critical, and he noted that the night mass meetings mustered a few hundred participants and that the daytime sessions never involved more than seventy-five delegates. Randolph's speech at the last meeting consisted of twenty-three typewritten pages, and he and his associates overwhelmingly voted for an all-Negro movement. Wilkins concluded that the movement consisted primarily of Randolph and members of the Brotherhood of Sleeping Car Porters, and he felt that the exclusion of whites was a serious mistake. He wrote, "The membership simply could

---

[30] "Proceedings from Conference Held in Detroit, September 26–27, 1942," p. 9. In NAACP Files, 1943 (270:3).

[31] NAACP Board of Directors Minutes, April 13, 1942. In NAACP Files, Series A, Box 11.

[32] NAACP Board of Directors Minutes, September 14, 1942. In NAACP Files, Series A, Box 11.

[33] Granger to Randolph, September 1, 1942. In National Urban League Files, Series I, Box 28. In April 1943, Granger objected strenuously to use of his name without authorization in a list of signatures to a letter to President Roosevelt. Randolph quickly apologized for what he said was an oversight resulting from haste. Granger to Randolph, April 13, 1943; Randolph to Granger, April 16, 1943. In National Urban League Files, Series I, Box 28.

not recognize the inconsistency involved in their protesting, for example, against lily-white labor unions and their advocacy of an all-Negro movement *against Jim Crow.*" Randolph's revival of the idea of an actual march on Washington was sharply criticized in the *Chicago Sun,* the only daily paper in Chicago friendly toward the conference.[34]

---

[34] "Memorandum to Mr. White from Mr. Wilkins" [caps], July 7, 1943 [the italics are Wilkins's]. In a supplementary report dated July 8, 1943, Wilkins wrote, "I am also informed that some white person described as a 'liberal' offered in March to contribute $150,000 to the Movement, with no strings attached. Randolph turned this down." Wilkins reported that the money was still available and that a showdown might develop between Randolph and those in the organization who wanted to accept the gift. In NAACP Files, 1943 (270:3). A copy of Randolph's speech is in this same box.

CHAPTER 3

Negro during Wartime: Government and Labor

THE FEDERAL GOVERNMENT poured millions of dollars into vocational training in an effort to gear the nation to war production. Initially, the percentage allotted to Negroes was small. Most of the money was used to retrain skilled workers and thus Negroes were left out—they needed training, not retraining.

The largest training program, the Vocational Educational National Defense (VEND), operated under the aegis of the Office of Education. Unfortunately, leadership at local and national levels was not interested in trying to alter the existing ideas involving racial discrimination. Educational leaders worked closely with business and labor unions, and neither encouraged the training of skilled Negro labor. Consequently, only 1.6 percent of 115,-000 trainees in preemployment and supplementary vocational education courses in December 1940 were Negroes.[1] More important, the few Negroes in training were mostly to be found in the North and even then few were trained in welding, machine shop, and aircraft work, where labor needs were greatest. Negroes were often admitted to courses involving nonessential training.

Negro leaders were aware that skilled manpower was needed in increasing numbers and that Negroes were denied a role proportionate to their percentage of the population. They thus sought to change the situation by bringing pressure to bear on representatives of federal agencies, industry, and labor at the local level to increase the training of Negro workers. The gains were slight in some cities, and in others where there was strong Negro leadership progress was made. For example, almost 25 percent of the enrollees in Detroit preemployment courses were Negro.

The Negro community had the additional task of persuading young people to enroll in the courses when they became eligible. Low-paying, unskilled positions were sometimes more desirable than nonpaying training courses even though the training would ultimately give the trainees an opportunity for better-paying jobs.

---

1 Robert C. Weaver, *Negro Labor: A National Problem* (New York: Harcourt, Brace, 1946), p. 45.

The task of introducing and expanding vocational training for Negroes in the South was much more difficult. Northern Negroes found it difficult to enter training courses, but once admitted they were placed in classes with whites. Vocational training in the South was segregated. There were few facilities for Negroes, and the process of expansion was extremely slow. The difference in facilities provided whites and Negroes was graphically illustrated in March 1941 in Birmingham, Alabama, where about 350 whites were enrolled in twenty-six different courses. They were trained in four high schools, all well equipped for teaching machine shop practice, welding, and drafting. In contrast, only one course (in blueprint reading) was open to Negroes, and it was conducted in a Negro industrial high school where the equipment consisted of one box of lead pencils and a few drawings. The director of defense training in Birmingham made no attempt to obtain federal funds. He and other vocational leaders in the South obviously questioned the training of Negroes to fill positions which would not be open to them even if they were skilled.

The federal government through the Office of Education had given Tennessee $230,000 for equipment for defense training by March 1941. Only $2,000 was used to fund courses for Negroes. The situation in Norfolk, Virginia, was exasperating to Negroes for another reason. The shipbuilding industry there, both federal and private, employed Negroes in unskilled and skilled positions, but Norfolk Negroes were forced to watch an influx of Negroes trained elsewhere take these positions. There were no training courses for Norfolk's Negro residents until the summer of 1942.[2]

The attitudes and apathy of officials in the Office of Education delayed Negro participation in war employment and thus hampered war production. The National Youth Administration, on the other hand, conscientiously tried to facilitate training young people, including Negroes. The NYA tried to establish nondiscriminatory policies and offered Negroes courses unavailable to them elsewhere. Mary McLeod Bethune, of the NYA, and other Negro leaders played a role in this case. Bethune undoubtedly influenced the NYA's decision to accept Negro women as enrollees long before other agencies did.

Negroes were encouraged by President Roosevelt's establishment of the FEPC and by the appointment to the committee of William Green and Philip Murray, heads of the AFL and the CIO, until it became evident that Green and Murray did not have time to at-

---

2 Weaver, *Negro Labor,* pp. 52–57. The examples cited are from this source.

tend the meetings. Frank Fenton (AFL) and John Brophy (CIO) were appointed as alternates.[3] David Sarnoff, head of Radio Corporation of America, who was known for his work on the New York governor's Committee on Discrimination, and two Negro members were also appointed. The appointment of Milton Webster, first international vice president of the Brotherhood of Sleeping Car Porters, was a tribute to the prestige of A. Philip Randolph; Earl B. Dickerson, alderman and member of the Chicago City Council, was the other Negro appointee.

Their experience illustrates the thin line that Negro leaders walked during the early war years. Milton Webster was outspoken and he frequently lectured his fellow committee members on human rights, but he presented his views within the committee.[4]

Dickerson was also outspoken, and on occasion he voiced different opinions outside the committee. Mark Ethridge opposed discrimination but defended segregation. He said, "There is no power in the world—not even in all the mechanized armies of the earth, Allied and Axis—which could now force the Southern white people to the abandonment of the principle of social segregation."[5] Dickerson publicly denounced Ethridge's statement as violating "both the letter and spirit of the President's Executive Order 8802." Dickerson asserted: "Because of the very nature of its creation, the Committee on Fair Employment Practice must be opposed to segregation and discrimination."[6] Dickerson was widely supported by the press; however, the committee adopted a policy wherein segregation would be considered a cause for complaint only when it contributed to discrimination.

Later, after the committee was placed under Paul V. McNutt (head of the War Manpower Commission), Dickerson, acting as chairman of the committee, issued an order without first clearing it with McNutt. The action resulted in the dissolution of the first committee, and the new committee created by President Roosevelt included Milton Webster but not Earl Dickerson.

The first FEPC was sharply limited by lack of funds and was

---

[3] Gunnar Myrdal, *An American Dilemma: The Negro Problem and Modern Democracy* (New York: Harper & Row, 1962), p. 503; Rackham Holt, *Mary McLeod Bethune: A Biography* (Garden City, N.Y.: Doubleday, 1964), p. 206.

[4] Malcolm Ross, *All Manner of Men* (New York: Greenwood Press, 1948), pp. 60–61.

[5] As quoted in Louis Coleridge Kesselman, *The Social Politics of FEPC: A Study in Reform Pressure Movements* (Chapel Hill: University of North Carolina Press, 1948), p. 169.

[6] As quoted in Louis Ruchames, *Race, Jobs, & Politics: The Story of FEPC* (New York: Columbia University Press, 1953), p. 41.

unable to set up branch offices throughout the country. The committee decided to institute a series of hearings to publicize its work by bringing cases of discrimination into the open. The committee thus proposed to use negotiation and public pressure to improve its situation. The committee conducted hearings in Los Angeles, Chicago, New York, and Birmingham during the period from October 1941 to June 1942.[7] In each hearing, the chairman began by defining the committee's background and objectives. Prominent local citizens and politicians would then speak, and representatives of minority groups were asked to present their grievances. Next, the committee would interrogate representatives of management and labor.

Following the first hearings held in Los Angeles, the committee offered recommendations for defense industries as a whole. Later the committee perceived that general admonitions were not enough and thereafter issued specific directives to industrial concerns and unions. Generally, the public and the press supported the committee. As expected, however, there was a notable lack of enthusiasm in the South for the Birmingham hearings.[8] After those hearings, President Roosevelt transferred the FEPC to the War Manpower Commission without explanation. The president's action was apparently motivated by pressure exerted by southern politicians. Despite his interest in extending civil rights and non-discrimination, Roosevelt's first obligation was to maintain full support for the war effort. He therefore could not risk alienating southern congressmen.

Roosevelt also needed the support of northern liberals who condemned the president's action, which they believed stifled the committee's efforts. Roosevelt explained that the transfer was not intended to inhibit the committee and that fair employment matters could still be referred to the president. The committee subsequently received greater financial support, but the revived optimism of its supporters did not last. The committee's decline began when McNutt postponed scheduled hearings on railroad cases. His action aroused the Negro press and other supporters, and a delegation representing several organizations visited McNutt in an effort to make him change his mind. McNutt refused

---

7 Ruchames, *Race, Jobs, & Politics*, pp. 27–28. For an example of Negro support of FEPC, see A. Philip Randolph to Edward S. Lewis, Executive Secretary, National Urban League, Baltimore, April 29, 1942. In Brotherhood of Sleeping Car Porters Records, Container No. 21.

8 Kesselman, *Social Politics of FEPC*, pp. 167–69.

to change his decision, several committee members resigned, and others were urged to quit in protest.

Roosevelt, alert to public opinion, announced that McNutt would meet with minority leaders to strengthen the committee. McNutt, Attorney General Francis Biddle, and other members of the administration accordingly met with representatives of some nineteen organizations on February 19, 1943. The administration declined to divulge its plans for the committee, and the minority leaders recommended that the FEPC be removed from the War Manpower Commission's jurisdiction and made responsible only to the president. Following this unsatisfactory meeting, the committee continued in limbo for several months while minority group leaders attempted to pressure the president into calling another conference. Nine leaders, including White, Granger, and Tobias, wrote President Roosevelt to demand action. Dickerson decided to act without McNutt's approval and announced that public hearings would be held in Detroit in May 1943 and later in St. Louis, Cleveland, Philadelphia, and Baltimore.

Dickerson's action resulted in termination of the committee. The White House requested the committee cancel the projected public hearings, and President Roosevelt issued Executive Order 9346 on May 27, 1943, which established a new FEPC, headed by Monsignor Francis J. Haas, dean of the School of Social Sciences at Catholic University. The first committee was a casualty but it had achieved two objectives. The new committee became an autonomous agency within the Office of Production Management but responsible only to the president. The budget of $80,000, originally assigned to the first committee, was increased to $500,-000, and a dozen branch offices were opened throughout the nation.

The new committee was first tested in a long series of hearings on railroad cases, initiated by the original committee, involving twenty-five railroads and fourteen unions. Monsignor Haas was reassigned by the church and resigned from the committee after the hearings but before the report was made public. Malcolm Ross replaced Haas and worked hard to eliminate discrimination.

The major issue in railroad cases was the Southeastern Carriers' Conference Agreement of February 18, 1941, which tended to perpetuate racial discrimination in the railroad industry. The committee made public the directives it sent to twenty railroad companies and seven labor unions on December 1, 1943, which ordered them to cease discrimination within thirty days. The committee announced that it would refer the matter to the president if the recipients failed to comply.

Generally the companies and unions were defiant—only two railroad companies announced intentions to comply. The signatories to the Southeastern Carriers' Conference Agreement refused to change its terms and declared that compliance with the FEPC directive would "result in stoppages of transportation, and would most gravely and irreparably impair the whole war effort of the country."[9] The committee had no alternative; the cases were forwarded to the president.

Again Roosevelt was forced to weigh social reform against the imperative of winning the war. He chose to take a delaying action and on January 3, 1944, announced the appointment of a special committee to examine the railroad cases. The committee included Chief Justice Walter P. Stacey of the supreme court of North Carolina, chairman; Judge William H. Holly of the federal district court of Chicago; and Frank J. Lausche, mayor of Cleveland, Ohio. The president instructed the committee to consider racial discrimination in all railroad positions except locomotive engineers and conductors—both traditionally white jobs.

The Stacey committee either failed to formulate a solution or the administration did not make it public. Malcolm Ross, chairman of the FEPC, subsequently recommended creation of a special committee, since he thought the president should not become personally involved. Ross later considered his recommendation a mistake in that he believed Roosevelt should have called managemen and labor together and used the presidency to end racial discrimination by the railroads.[10] Yet it is doubtful that the president would have done so because railroad transportation was too important to the conduct of the war. Antidiscrimination again lost out in the contest of priorities.

The FEPC's stand on the railroads was confirmed by the Supreme Court in two decisions handed down in December 1944. In *Steele v. Louisville and Nashville Railroad Company* and *Tunstall v. Brotherhood of Locomotive Firemen and Enginemen,* the Court held that a labor union acting as a bargaining agent for

---

9 Letter, Atlantic Coast Line Railroad and other companies to President's Committee on Fair Employment Practice, December 13, 1943 [mimeographed]. In NAACP Files, 1943 (275:1). For a good summary, see Ruchames, *Race, Jobs, & Politics,* pp. 46–56. See also Herbert Garfinkel, *When Negroes March: The March on Washington Movement in the Organizational Politics for FEPC* (Glencoe, Ill.: Free Press, 1959), pp. 148–49.

10 Ross, *All Manner of Men,* p. 132.

an entire class of workers could not enter into an agreement which discriminated against some of the workers on account of race. Despite these decisions, the Southeastern Carriers' Conference Agreement continued in practice for several years.

The FEPC evoked opposition from Congress. A congressional committee was appointed to investigate acts of executive agencies that were beyond their authority, and it regarded the FEPC as a prime object of inquiry. The ensuing investigations of the FEPC irritated committee members. The investigations probably encouraged some businesses to violate committee directives, but the agency was not discredited. The speeches made in Congress by opponents of the FEPC made for an uncomfortable existence, but they did not prevent the committee from functioning as a wartime agency. Mainly, its opponents sought to prevent the FEPC from becoming a permanent institution.[11]

The FEPC became interested in the urban transit industry and Negro rights increased somewhat during the war. Employment as platform operators (motormen, conductors, and bus drivers) was appealing to Negroes because many such positions were needed to operate mass transit systems and because these positions had greater visibility and status than unskilled labor. Also the training requirements involved little time and were relatively easy to meet.

Consequently, it became difficult to explain why Negroes could not qualify for job openings. Negroes also noted that most supervisors worked up through the ranks, so platform positions appeared to offer Negro job seekers opportunities for advancement. Since many transit systems were publicly owned, Negroes felt these were more susceptible to public pressure than was private industry.[12]

The hiring of Negroes in the urban transit industry did not represent a steady advance nationwide, rather, hiring practices varied from city to city. There were three separate transit systems in New York City before 1940, and all of them employed the majority of Negro workers as porters. A few Negroes were advanced to other positions during the 1930s, and the Transport Workers Union (CIO) was largely responsible for the hiring of a few Negro conductors and station agents during vacation periods. In 1935

11 See Ruchames, *Race, Jobs, & Politics*, pp. 87–99.

12 Philip W. Jeffress, *The Negro in the Urban Transit Industry*, The Racial Policies of American Industry, Report No. 18 (Philadelphia: University of Pennsylvania Press, 1970), pp. 24–25.

the Independent Subway System admitted Negroes to competitive civil service examinations—the process through which appointments and promotions were made. The Board of Aldermen opened positions to all applicants, and this important move encouraged other transit companies in the city to accept the idea of open civil service examinations. Open examinations were continued when the unified New York City Transit System was created in 1940, following the bankruptcy of the three separate systems. By December 1943, 9.4 percent of the workers in the transit industry were nonwhite, and of these 6.9 percent were operators. By January 1945, more Negroes were employed in important transit jobs in New York than in any other city in the country.

Detroit, however, led in the initial employment of Negroes in other than menial positions in the transit industry after the city took over municipal ownership and operation of the urban transit system in 1922. At that time, appointments in other branches of city government were made through competitive civil service examinations. The same rule applied to urban transit positions, opening the way for Negro employment. Two decades later, in December 1943, 25.8 percent of the employees in the urban transit industry were Negro, and 27.4 percent were employed as operators. New York and Detroit were ahead of other cities at the time.

Nevertheless, a break in the pattern of nonemployment of Negroes was to appear in Chicago. The data for Detroit and New York[13] revealed there was only one Negro operator in Chicago in 1943. The change during the next few months was initiated by the manager of the Chicago Surface Lines in cooperation with a leader of the AFL Amalgamated Union of Streetcar Workers, who favored nondiscrimination and won union support for the change. Public meetings helped dispel initial fear of an adverse public reaction or a strike, and Negroes were introduced as operators without incident. By August 1944, 140 were in service.

The road toward Negro employment was not as smooth in Los Angeles. The Negro press there campaigned for the hiring of Negro operators by transit lines; Negro civic organizations and the local leader of one of the streetcar unions supported the campaign. The complaints of the local union brought in the War Manpower Commission and the FEPC, which arranged a meeting between the management and labor representatives. The labor leader, who

---

13 Jeffress, *The Negro in the Urban Transit Industry*, p. 26.

argued for the hiring of Negroes, was opposed by his union. The company agreed to upgrade two Negroes, and eighty white employees responded with a work stoppage, forcing the company to cease hiring Negro operators. The liberal union leader subsequently lost a union election, and the company made no further attempt to upgrade Negroes for some time. At hearings held by the FEPC in August 1944 in Los Angeles the transit situation was discussed, since it was found that the two transit companies there did not employ Negro operators. Executives of the Los Angeles Railway Company defended their discriminatory policy by noting that work stoppages had occurred.

The manpower needs of the war sustained the position of both sides. Proponents of hiring Negroes stressed that many Negroes were available for work while buses were standing idle during peak hours for lack of drivers. They argued that Negroes should be hired to improve vital transportation services in time of war. Opponents of Negro employment threatened mass transportation stoppages if Negroes were hired and upgraded. The threat to the seniority system was also used to argue against hiring Negroes. These counterarguments appeared at local levels everywhere, in connection with the employment of Negroes on the railroads. Following the public hearings, the FEPC met informally with company and union representatives and persuaded the transit company to issue a nondiscrimination directive. By March 20, 1945, seventy-four Negro operators were employed, Negroes in shops and garages were upgraded without problem, and the fear of work stoppages proved to be a chimera.[14]

The success in Los Angeles was not repeated in Oakland, California, despite the FEPC hearings and recommendations. Negroes were not hired as operators in the Key System Transit Lines. The local union controlled employment in this system, and Negroes were kept out by refusals to admit them to union membership. This state of affairs continued until the 1950s.

The hiring of Negroes in the transit industry in Philadelphia was even more complicated. From 1911 to 1937, management controlled labor and there was even a company union. The union was declared illegal in 1937 and was replaced by the Philadelphia Rapid Transit Employees Union (PRTEU), which was nominally independent but still actually dominated by the company. The AFL and CIO entered the picture and the workers voted in March 1944 to determine which union would become their bargaining

---

[14] Jeffress, *The Negro in the Urban Transit Industry*, pp. 30–33.

agent. The Transport Workers Union won with 55 percent of the vote.

Prior to the election the FEPC had ordered the company and the PRTEU to follow nondiscriminatory hiring policies. The union responded that the FEPC was attempting to destroy the seniority system of the Philadelphia Transportation Company. The FEPC repeated its directive when the Transport Workers Union became the bargaining agent and the emphasis shifted to the issue of union leadership. The deposed PRTEU officials fought vigorously to unseat the Transport Workers Union and precipitated a strike, which started on the morning of August 1 in the streetcar system and spread to bus drivers and other operators. It is estimated that not more than 200 persons actively supported the strike, but they moved shrewdly and quickly to tie up the city's transit system. Company officials made no effort to prevent the strike or to stop it. The mayor was indecisive and the workers, aside from the hard-core strike leadership, were unsympathetic. Workers were diverted by the charge that their seniority was endangered by Negro upgradings, and this issue rather than Negro employment per se concerned them.

The Transport Workers Union, which nominally represented the workers, opposed the strike from the beginning. Company officials sought to suspend the rules on nondiscrimination as a way of ending the strike. The War Manpower Commission and FEPC, however, refused the company permission to proceed and instead referred the matter to the president.

The public generally denounced the strike, and workers were soon placed on the defensive for impeding the war effort. Several hundred of them planned to return to work on August 3 but changed their minds when city police failed to appear and protect them. That evening President Roosevelt ordered the army to assume control of the city transit system, and army officials announced that the policies on nondiscrimination pronounced when the strike started would be upheld. Workers delayed returning to work, and the army command sternly admonished them, making it clear that workers were ordered, not advised, to return to work. The arrest of four strike leaders emphasized that the army meant business, and the strike was ended. A few Negroes began training, and by mid-August seven were on the job. There was no opposition, more Negroes were hired, and the army left the city on August 17. The company fired the four strike leaders who had been arrested, and the workers voted to increase their support of the Transport Workers Union.

The Philadelphia transit case was a victory for the federal agencies involved in the struggle against discrimination. Their strong stand in Philadelphia apparently set an example which helped end the controversy in urban transit in Los Angeles.

The most conspicuous failure of the FEPC in urban transit matters occurred in the nation's capital. In 1934 the threat of a strike was sufficient to check the employment of Negroes as operators by the Capital Transit Company. The company resisted hiring Negroes and resorted to other expedients to solve the labor shortage induced by the war. Two-man cars were converted to one-man cars; white women were trained and employed as operators in preference to Negro men. The company position was strongly supported by southern congressmen, and their support no doubt encouraged the company to avoid changes in policy even after the FEPC hearings held in January 1945. After the war, in November 1945, the union went on strike in Washington, and President Truman seized the transit facilities. Despite the urgings of FEPC, Truman failed to force the company and the union to cease racial discrimination. The company continued to discriminate against Negroes until 1956, when new franchise owners took over and adopted a policy of nondiscrimination.[15] In summary, the FEPC was more successful in combating discrimination in urban transit cases than in most other areas of employment despite the setbacks in Oakland and Washington.

Negro employment during World War II generally resulted from a combination of four factors: a demand for increased production; a shortage in the labor supply; the intervention of government agencies, notably the FEPC; and the pressure applied by Negroes and others interested in ending discrimination. The first two factors were decisive. In the petroleum industry, for example, "economics proved to be more effective than government action," and in the meat industry the rise of Negro employment resulted from an increase in industry and a decrease of white labor.[16]

The most dramatic shift resulting from these factors came in the aerospace industry, which was a particular target of the Negro

---

15 Jeffress, *The Negro in the Urban Transit Industry,* pp. 38–40. For an example of the FEPC's lack of success with labor unions, see Thurgood Marshall, "Negro Status in the Boilermakers Union," *Crisis* 51 (March 1944): 77.

16 Carl B. King and Howard W. Risher, Jr., *The Negro in the Petroleum Industry,* The Racial Policies of American Industry, Report No. 5 (Philadelphia: University of Pennsylvania Press, 1969), p. 32; Walter A. Fogel, *The Negro in the Meat Industry,* The Racial Policies of American Industry, Report No. 12 (Philadelphia: University of Pennsylvania Press, 1970), pp. 52–53.

press early in the war. Aerospace managers had a penchant for making clearly discriminatory statements. The president of North American Aviation, Inc., advised a group of Negro leaders that the new bomber plant in Kansas City would ". . . receive applications from both white and Negro workers. However, the Negroes will be considered only as janitors and in other similar capacities."[17] Glenn Martin, an aviation pioneer, said that it was impracticable to employ Negroes, since white workers might go out on strike.[18] The head of Vultee stated, "It is not the policy of this company to employ people other than of the Caucasian race."[19] The Los Angeles hearings of the FEPC brought these discriminatory practices into the open. Douglas, North American, and Lockheed-Vega were among the companies represented at the hearings.[20]

Because the penetration of the aircraft industry by Negro workers varied considerably from place to place, it is difficult to cite typical cases. The Boeing Company in Seattle, for example, decided to do business with organized labor unions. One of them, the International Association of Machinists (AFL), controlled hiring in the Boeing plant. This union excluded Negroes from membership, and that rule enabled management to blame discriminatory hiring on union policy. The Seattle Urban League pressured the company and union, only to be denounced as Communist. Negroes were excluded from training courses and thus further blocked in their attempts to find jobs.

The situation came to the attention of the FEPC, which proved incapable of resolving the issue, and the entire matter was referred to the president. Roosevelt's administration convinced union leaders that they should issue permits for Negroes to work, but the local branch delayed its response to the directives of its international officers. However, the demand for production and an adequate labor force was too strong. Negroes who were local residents were employed by Boeing beginning in mid-1942, and the residence restriction was later removed.[21]

Lockheed-Vega provides the best example of management support for Negro employment. The president of the corporation

---

17 As quoted in Herbert R. Northrup, *The Negro in the Aerospace Industry*, The Racial Policies of American Industry, Report No. 2 (Philadelphia: University of Pennsylvania Press, 1968), p. 19.

18 Northrup, *The Negro in the Aerospace Industry*, p. 19.

19 As quoted in Weaver, *Negro Labor*, p. 109.

20 Ruchames, *Race, Jobs, & Politics*, pp. 160–61.

21 Weaver, *Negro Labor*, pp. 116–17.

wrote to the Office of Production Management in the spring of 1941 and advised that agency that the company was studying the hiring of Negroes. The corporate secretary wrote all of the executives and supervisors in August to draw attention to President Roosevelt's Executive Order 8802. The memorandum noted that the company did not have "any discriminatory policies with regard to race, color or creed" but that it employed no Negroes and that the company would comply with Roosevelt's directive. Finally, the letter asked for the support of employers. The management informed the employees concerning those developments, and the supervisors were cooperative. Lockheed-Vega employed more than 300 Negroes in various jobs by February. At the end of the year over 1,000 Negro workers, including women, were employed. In mid-1944, 5 percent of the work force was Negro.[22]

Overall, the percentage of Negroes employed in the aircraft industry was slightly higher than in Seattle, and the proportion increased from .2 of 1 percent in 1940 to about 6 percent by the summer of 1944. Robert C. Weaver summarized the situation: "It resulted, as all increases in Negro employment in war production, principally from the tightness of the labor market and the attempts to enforce the executive orders banning discrimination in defense employment."[23]

The automobile industry was different—it was older and Negroes had already made progress. The shift to production of war materials, tanks, aircraft, and trucks was initially discriminatory, since management was sometimes reluctant to train Negroes, in fear of alienating the white labor force. The Ford Motor Company led the way and unhesitatingly retrained Negro workers without waiting for governmental admonitions.

The retraining and upgrading of Negroes in the industry resulted in protests and work stoppages. Some plants refused to retrain Negroes, thus evoking vigorous protests from pressure groups. Other plants attempted to retrain Negroes, which resulted in work stoppages and threats of strike. The most serious strike occurred in June 1943 in the Detroit Packard plant, the scene of labor trouble several times during the preceding few years. The strike began because of the upgrading of Negroes, and it aroused opposition from unions, management, and government. Their combined efforts broke the strike within a week.[24]

---

22 Weaver, *Negro Labor*, pp. 196–99.
23 Weaver, *Negro Labor*, p. 121.
24 From the NAACP Emergency War Conference in session in Detroit,

Negroes made significant progress in the automotive industry during World War II despite many recurring problems. Chrysler, by the end of the war, had the largest percentage of Negroes employed in the industry. General Motors employed the first Negro apprentices in its Oldsmobile plant. Briggs, which became a subsidiary of the Chrysler division, was the first to hire numbers of Negro women in various types of work.[25]

As the war ended, Negroes proudly noted their contribution to building the huge war machine so important to the eventual victory. Millions of Negroes participated in war work, and many held positions formerly denied to them. Yet, the greatest success was achieved where labor demands were the greatest and white workers in short supply. Negroes broadened their scope of employment in the South, but their gains were mostly slight. For example, the aircraft industry reversed itself and hired Negroes in plants everywhere but in the South. The Vultee plant in Fort Worth, Texas, refused to train Negroes until near the end of the war,[26] and most Negroes employed in southern industries were restricted to unskilled labor. Only 5 percent of the work force in the rubber industry was Negro, and when management tried to employ Negroes as skilled labor the white workers threatened to strike, ending that effort. Meat packing plants and oil refineries employed Negroes in unskilled jobs formerly closed to them.[27]

The gains made during the war did not make Negroes overly optimistic about their futures. Robert C. Weaver reminded them: "The upgrading of Negroes and the industrial employment of Negro women are not social experiments. They are wartime economic necessities."[28] Many leaders realized that Negroes would be exposed to the ancient practice, "last hired, first fired," as the war

Walter White sent a telegram to President Roosevelt, June 4, 1943, urging him to "issue orders to take over Packard Plant here." In NAACP Files, 1943 (275:5). The increased interest of the NAACP in labor was shown by the assignment of Prentice Thomas, Assistant Special Counsel, to work on labor relations. Thomas wrote to a number of persons and agencies for information. See NAACP Files, 1943 (270:2).

25 Herbert R. Northrup, *The Negro in the Automobile Industry*, The Racial Policies of American Industry, Report No. 1 (Philadelphia: University of Pennsylvania Press, 1968), pp. 18–20.

26 Weaver, *Negro Labor*, p. 115. See also Northrup, *The Negro in the Aerospace Industry*, p. 20.

27 Herbert R. Northrup, *The Negro in the Rubber Tire Industry*, The Racial Policies of American Industry, Report No. 6 (Philadelphia: University of Pennsylvania Press, 1969), p. 38; Fogel, *The Negro in the Meat Industry*, p. 53; King and Risher, *The Negro in the Petroleum Industry*, pp. 32–34.

28 Robert C. Weaver, "The Negro Comes of Age in Industry," in Bucklin Moon, *Primer for White Folks* (New York: Doubleday, Doran, 1945), p. 449.

industries came to an end. The Department of Labor warned in January 1945 that "the Negro has made his greatest employment gains in those occupations (especially semiskilled factory jobs) which will suffer the severest cutbacks during the postwar period." The report further noted that Negroes had made their greatest advances "in those industries (especially the 'metals, chemicals, and rubber' groups) which will experience the greatest post-war declines."[29]

Nonetheless, Negroes hoped that the myth of Negro inferiority could be laid to rest. Trained Negroes in plants all over the country had matched the best efforts of their white counterparts. The stereotype of the Negro laborer as a strikebreaker had also been shattered, since Negroes and whites in organized labor realized that the key to success lay in unity rather than discord.[30] Negro leaders like Robert C. Weaver came to realize that Negro prospects were best if they were joined with the betterment of the entire economy instead of concentrated on improvements for the Negro. Consequently, Negro leaders began to stress full employment as a goal after the war.

---

[29] As quoted in Richard L. Rowan, *The Negro in the Steel Industry*, The Racial Policies of American Industry, Report No. 3 (Philadelphia: University of Pennsylvania Press, 1968), p. 38.

[30] James S. Olson, "Race, Class, and Progress: Black Leadership and Industrial Unionism, 1936–1945," in Milton Cantor, ed., *Black Labor in America* (Westport, Conn.: Negro Universities Press, 1969), pp. 163–64. The CIO appointed a Negro literary figure, Roi Ottley, as Director, Public Information, National CIO Committee for American and Allied War Relief. See Ottley to Roy Wilkins, May 13, 1943. In NAACP Files, 1943 (270:2).

CHAPTER 4

Prototype 1943:
Long, Hot Summer

DURING WORLD WAR II millions of Americans left their normal ways of life to do things they never dreamed of doing; they became soldiers instead of students, war workers instead of garage mechanics, lawyers, and housewives. Millions left their homes and moved to unfamiliar parts of the country, often to inferior housing. Their plans for the future were deferred and, indeed, most doubted that their lives would ever be the same again.

These often traumatic readjustments were accepted when the war started, largely because of the patriotic fervor which involved most people. Some people were also motivated by desire for fame, status, excitement, or a change from the tedium of their daily existence. Others accepted the changes for monetary gain—war wages were comparatively high. The early enthusiasm tended to fade as the war went on, and people began to accept the idea that there was a job to be done. The growing casualty lists showed that the companion of fame could be death, working at routine work on a night shift was often dull and exhausting, and the family home often occupied the memories of people cooped up in strange cities and congested housing. In addition, Negroes generally were not getting their fair share of anything—fame, work, or housing.

Tensions rose to the point of violence in several American cities during the long, hot summer of 1943. The first violence occurred in Los Angeles and involved Negroes only incidentally. The population of Los Angeles grew faster than that of most cities during the war, and the city's minority problems increased accordingly. A quarter of a million people of Mexican descent—a fourth of them Mexican nationals and the remainder citizens of the United States—were living in squalor and congestion. They were victims of discrimination, living in an environment conducive to juvenile delinquency and crime. The growth of war industries brought thousands of Negroes into the Los Angeles basin. The Negroes were forced into segregated housing and many poured into "Little Tokyo," a section left by the evacuated Japanese. Some Mexican, Negro, and other youths formed gangs in Los Angeles. By the summer of 1943 the zoot suit, which originated in Harlem, was

adopted by Mexican youths to symbolize their membership in
"pachuco" gangs. The "zoot-suiter" had been described as "a
youth wearing a flat hat with a very wide brim, a jacket that
swept low, pants that started out under the armpits, bagged out
at the knees and tied in at the ankles, a watch chain that threatened to trip its wearer, and shoes sharply pointed and with thick
soles."[1]

Los Angeles became a great war production center, and it attracted thousands of soldiers and sailors on leave from nearby
military posts. The influx of sailors created friction with some of
the gangs, often because of competition for the company of young
women. The pachuco gangs attacked sailors in streets and alleys,
and the sailors returned in groups to raid portions of the city.
They would search out gang members, tear off their distinctive
apparel, and subject them to other indignities. The pachucos
fought back and the battles aroused national concern. Finally
and belatedly, the officials intervened. Army and navy commanders canceled military leaves and briefly placed Los Angeles off
limits for military personnel not on duty. The gang war disturbances exemplified the kind of ethnic frictions arising from congested urban conditions in a nation at war. They were the result
of conflicts that arose between youngsters in crowded, low economic and social areas and servicemen with too much time on
their hands. Negroes were peripherally involved when they were
occasionally mistaken for pachucos and thus mistreated.[2]

A more serious development occurred in Detroit, where there
were all the ingredients for a riot. The population of over 1,600,-
000 included 500,000 southern whites and 210,000 Negroes, mostly
from the South. Detroit boomed in the twenties with the rise of
the automobile industry and suffered one of the first and worst
"busts" during the depression. It was a city of rabble-rousers, a
"religious-political-agitational crowd."[3] More than 2,500 southern
evangelists were reported in the area, and they operated their own

---

1 *New York Times*, June 13, 1943.

2 Julius A. Thomas, "Race Conflict and Social Action," *Opportunity* 21
(October 1943): 166; Chester B. Himes, "Zoot Riots Are Race Riots," *Crisis*
50 (July 1943): 200–201, 222. Walter White wrote a letter to President Roosevelt and members of his cabinet on the "zoot suit" disturbances. White to
President Roosevelt, Secretary Stimson, Secretary Knox, Attorney General
Biddle, June 11, 1943. In NAACP Files, 1943 (291:4). His recommendations
were not unlike recommendations made by an investigating committee called
by Governor Earl Warren and headed by Joseph T. McGucken. See its report,
dated June 12, 1943. In NAACP Files, 1943 (291:4).

3 Earl Brown, "The Truth about the Detroit Riot," *Harper's Magazine*
(November 1943): 491.

churches and tent tabernacles—sometimes, on a part-time basis, they held jobs in industry. Some churches were fronts for the Ku Klux Klan. Evangelists included J. Frank Norris, from Alabama by way of Texas, whose preaching was described as "the standard sulphurous gospel of Southern tradition, but in excelsis."[4] Gerald L. K. Smith was more widely known; he had received some political training in Louisiana from Huey Long. Father Coughlin, Smith's Catholic counterpart, had already built a wide radio following.[5]

Negroes in Detroit were grouped into social categories. The masses were jammed into crowded, almost unlivable slums. More prosperous Negroes escaped to little islands of separatism in middle-class white areas of the city. The first black settlers were not welcomed by the whites.

A highly publicized incident occurred during the mid-1920s; a Negro doctor, Ossian Sweet, shot into a mob that was stoning his home. Clarence Darrow subsequently won Sweet's release in a sensational trial. Negroes and whites alike had rough and criminal elements, young toughs, and racketeers. The profitable policy racket run by Negroes could not have succeeded without their paying off white city officials.

The war intensified everything—job opportunities, housing shortages, and interracial hostility. Detroit had experienced high tensions and violence prior to the summer of 1943. For example, a crisis arose over housing early in 1942. Living accommodations were hard to find, especially for Negroes, since they were forced to pay much higher rents than whites for miserable facilities and they were excluded from war defense housing. The federal government had begun constructing a housing project for Negroes in 1941 in an area located between Negro and white sections. The whites believed the property belonged to them. A group of Polish residents opposed the building of homes for Negroes in "their" area, got the support of the local congressman, picketed city hall, and petitioned the Federal Housing Administration in Washington. That agency announced that the project, already named Sojourner Truth after the ex-slave heroine of the Civil War, would be open only to whites. This action was too much for Mayor Edward Jeffries and he protested, "That would be tantamount to saying to the Negroes that there is no place within the

---

4 Brown, "Truth about the Detroit Riot," p. 490.
5 Robert Shogan and Tom Craig, *The Detroit Race Riot: A Study in Violence* (Philadelphia: Chilton Books, 1964), p. 27.

city where they can have new housing."[6] The federal agency
yielded and reversed its decision. Negroes then paid their rents in
advance, loaded their household belongings into vans, and prepared to move into their new apartments on February 28. White
crowds met the vans and forcibly prevented their unloading. The
police at the scene made no effort to protect the Negroes and actually tended to prevent them from moving in.[7] A Negro driver
was hit by a stone, but there were no serious injuries. Negro
spokesmen subsequently charged that the Ku Klux Klan and the
National Workers' League (reputedly a Nazi front organization)
had instigated the opposition, but no action was taken. The
Negro families moved into the Sojourner Truth housing project
two months later with the support of state and local police.

An event in Detroit following that hopeful outcome indicated
that it was still possible to express differences of opinion. The
labor committee of the NAACP and the interracial committee of
the United Automobile Workers (UAW-CIO) demonstrated in
Cadillac Square on Sunday, April 11, in protest over the slow
utilization of Negro men and women in war work. A parade of
5,000 people—Boy Scouts, majorettes, air raid wardens, an American Legion drum and bugle corps, and a women's volunteer
corps unit—attracted a crowd of 10,000 to the square, where they
listened to white and Negro speakers describe Negro needs and
accomplishments.[8] However, in May the upgrading of Negro
workers in the Packard plant produced a flare-up similar to others
at the Ford and Vickers plants. These were not major eruptions,
merely indications of growing racial tensions.

An investigating team, sent by the Office of Facts and Figures
to Detroit after the Sojourner Truth project affair, predicted,
"This country, or let us say the war effort, will face its greatest
crisis all over the North." The investigators noted that racial discrimination was a problem nationwide and concluded that if
"strong and quick intervention by some high official, preferably
the President, is not taken at once, hell is going to be let loose in
every Northern city where large numbers of immigrants and Negroes are in competition."[9] The investigators felt that Mayor
Jeffries of Detroit was not strong enough to handle the situation
in his city and that the federal government should step in, prom-

6 As quoted in Shogan and Craig, *Detroit Race Riot*, p. 115.
7 Gunnar Myrdal, *An American Dilemma: The Negro Problem and Modern Democracy* (New York: Harper & Row, 1962), p. 1337.
8 *Crisis* 50 (May 1943): 154.
9 As quoted in Shogan and Craig, *Detroit Race Riot*, p. 31.

ise adequate housing for all, and announce at the same time that racial violence would not be permitted. This report was not made public, and on the surface it appeared that nothing had happened to disrupt the city.

Walter White received a disturbing letter from Leslie Perry, of the Washington bureau of the NAACP, early in May:[10]

> I understand that Walter Reuther and R. J. Thomas are very much concerned about the race situation in Detroit. It appears that Negroes are in a position to close down three or four shops there and are threatening to do so simply because they are generally mad about everything.

The labor leaders were disturbed because the threats disrupted efforts "to get Negroes into the shops" and because wildcat strikes would hurt the United Automobile Workers. Perry also commented on the attitudes of Reuther and Thomas toward the March on Washington:[11]

> They feel that the all-Negro character of the March on Washington intensifies the wrong type of racial consciousness and have gone to Phil Randolph and told him to tone it down and make it interracial.

White thanked Perry for the information and responded, "It sounds almost unbelievable, but I am asking Thurgood [Marshall] to look into it, since he is leaving for Detroit tomorrow."[12]

Despite Perry's report on racial tensions, the NAACP, in tune with racial discord as much as any national group, held a scheduled conference in Detroit from June 3 to 6. The main concern of the conference seemed to be the role of the Negro in the armed forces. The delegates adopted a statement that decried the treatment of Negroes in the armed services and in industry. There were strong presentations of Negro points of view, but the conference was essentially temperate. By the time the NAACP's *Crisis* published its July issue, the conference had become back-page news.[13]

---

10 Leslie Perry to Walter White, May 4, 1943. In NAACP Files, 1943 (270:1).
11 Perry to White, May 4, 1943.
12 White to Perry, May 10, 1943. In NAACP Files, 1943 (270:1).
13 For reports on the conference, see NAACP Board of Directors Minutes, June 14, 1943, p. 3; July 12, 1943, p. 2. In NAACP Files, Series A, Box 11. Robert C. Weaver wrote to Walter White congratulating him on the Detroit meeting: "I was pleasantly surprised by the 17,000 persons who must have been present." Weaver to White, June 7, 1943. In NAACP Files, 1943 (275:5). President Roosevelt sent his greetings as he had the previous year. Roosevelt to White, May 24, 1943; July 7, 1942. In NAACP Files, 1943 (275:5).

The Detroit riot was on the front page. The ingredients for riot mentioned earlier came together in a violent explosion on the evening of June 20, 1943. The weather was a factor—a steaming 91 degrees that Sunday afternoon. Most Negroes lived in Paradise Valley—a thirty-block ghetto with vile living accommodations and no decent recreational facilities. Many Negroes left the ghetto that day to visit Belle Isle, a small island in the Detroit River, the only accessible park available to them. During the afternoon Belle Isle became crowded with at least 100,000 people, most of them Negroes. Negro and white youths started a small fight, which quickly escalated into one of the worst race riots in American history. When it was over, twenty-five Negroes and nine white persons were dead.[14]

Within about an hour and a half, the fight had expanded across the access bridge into Paradise Valley, and police reservists failed to check the fighting, which involved an estimated 5,000 people. Negro mobs fanned out three miles north of Paradise Valley and attacked individual whites. Meanwhile, stores in the Negro ghetto were looted and smashed. News of the disturbance included wild rumors about the killing of whites and Negroes. White groups began to retaliate in force at about 4 A.M. while the mayor, the police commissioner, and other officials met in a hurried council. Colonel A. M. Kreck, army commander of the Detroit area, assured the mayor that military police battalions could be dispatched within forty-nine minutes after a request had gone from the mayor through the governor to the proper army officials. The mayor, encouraged by a report that the rioting was dying down, took no action. The report was false and the rioting continued.

A Negro delegation persuaded the mayor to attend a biracial meeting early on the morning of the twenty-first, and shortly afterwards the police commissioner asked Mayor Jeffries to phone Governor Harry F. Kelly and ask the army to send in troops. The governor declined to proclaim martial law, an act requisite to calling in the troops. The rioting continued and groups of white hoodlums roamed the streets, overturning cars and attacking Negroes.

At noon an interracial meeting was held, and R. J. Thomas, president of the UAW-CIO, vigorously demanded that steps be taken to end the rioting. The governor and the commanding general in the area flew to Detroit for consultations while lootings,

---

14 Brown, "Truth about the Detroit Riot," p. 488. See Alfred McClung Lee and Norman Daymond Humphrey, *Race Riot* (New York: Dryden Press, 1943), pp. 83–84, and detailed chronology of the riot.

beatings, and other acts of violence continued. Four white youths shot and killed a 58-year-old Negro, and one of them explained they had murdered "just for the Hell of it." One of the boys said, "We didn't know him. He wasn't bothering us. But other people were fighting and killing and we felt like it, too."[15] Governor Kelly proclaimed a state of "modified martial law" early in the evening, but his decree did not meet the requirements for calling in federal troops. Finally at 9:25 P.M., the governor called President Roosevelt and asked for troops to end the riot. The president directed the troops to restore order and asked the people to desist from further violence. The soldiers had already moved in, and by that time the rioting had practically spent itself; so the troops did not have to fire a shot.

Reactions to the riot were vigorous in Detroit and throughout the nation. R. J. Thomas called for "immediate and effective community reaction" to prevent new outbreaks.[16] The press and members of Congress blamed various individuals for the riot. The editor of the *Jackson* [Miss.] *Daily News* blamed Eleanor Roosevelt; Congressman John E. Rankin of Mississippi announced that the culprit was the FEPC.[17] Congressman Martin Dies of the House Un-American Activities Committee determined that Japanese-Americans were the real instigators, and he had to be dissuaded from taking his committee to Detroit to investigate.[18] Most people blamed either Negroes or whites, depending on their point of view.

The rioting covered large parts of the city and involved thousands of people, but whole sections remained virtually untouched. Generally it was found that Negroes and whites who knew one another or who worked together did not participate in the violence. Men of both races continued to work side by side in war plants during the riot, which nonetheless took its toll in absenteeism, wasted man-hours, and money. Negro and white students at Wayne State University attended classes together on Monday during the riot.

The Detroit riot did not receive an extensive, objective analysis like that which followed the Chicago outburst of 1919. The Detroit City Council rejected a request for a grand jury investigation. Mayor Jeffries issued an apologia on June 30 in which he explained the delay in obtaining federal troops, stated that he

---

15 As quoted in Lee and Humphrey, *Race Riot*, pp. 37–38.
16 Lee and Humphrey, *Race Riot*, p. 46.
17 Shogan and Craig, *Detroit Race Riot*, p. 98.
18 Brown, "Truth about the Detroit Riot," p. 497.

objected to martial law because "civil functions would be completely abrogated," and praised the police. The mayor's statement
angered the local NAACP, and Dr. James J. McClendon, its president, protested: "We do not condone the acts of hoodlums of our
race, any more than you condone those who turned over cars,"
but, he continued, "it takes no crystal gazer to add the number
of Negroes slain by the police or compare the lack of such 'shoot
to kill' policy on Woodward Avenue [against white persons]."[19]
Seventeen of the twenty-five Negroes who died were shot by the
police.[20]

The Columbia Broadcasting System focused national attention
on the Detroit riot in a radio broadcast on July 24, 1943, repeated
in half-hour programs nationwide. The "CBS Open Letter on
Race Hatred" was a hard-hitting documentary which ended with
a postscript by Wendell Wilkie. He characterized the motivation
of rioters as "the same basic motivation as actuates the fascist
mind when it seeks to dominate whole people and nations."[21]
The following day 15,000 whites and Negroes listened to a speech
given at the state fairgrounds just outside Detroit by Vice President Henry Wallace, who declared that "we cannot fight to crush
Nazi brutality abroad and condone race riots at home."[22] Charges
and countercharges continued in Detroit for several days. The
county prosecutor and the police commissioner blamed a group of
young Negroes on Belle Isle for starting the riot and the Negro

19 Jeffries, as quoted in Lee and Humphrey, *Race Riot*, p. 55; McClendon's
response is quoted on p. 56.

20 Shogan and Craig, *Detroit Race Riot*, pp. 130–31. A study made some
time later of the 97 Negroes and 8 white men "convicted of felonies and in-
carcerated in State prisons" as a result of the Detroit riot reached the following conclusions: The men were "disproportionately natives of States south of
the Mason and Dixon line." They were educationally inferior and generally
unskilled workmen. "Seventy-four percent of the riot group had previously
been in conflict with the law-enforcing agencies. Twenty-three of this number
had prison records." Most of the men had been sentenced as looters and carriers of concealed weapons and not for active and violent participation in the
riot. See Elmer R. Akers and Vernon Fox, "The Detroit Rioters and Looters
Committed to Prison" [10 pp. carbon, typewritten]. In NAACP Files, 1944
(291:4).

21 As quoted in Lee and Humphrey, *Race Riot*, p. 64. The Columbia Broadcasting System had been interested in the Negro and the war for some time.
In April 1942, Leigh White of CBS and Walter White of NAACP corresponded
about a proposed meeting to discuss counteracting Nazi and Japanese propaganda which was making use of the racial issues in the United States. See
Leigh White to Walter White, April 29, 1942, and Walter White to Leigh
White, April 29, 1942, and folder on Nazi propaganda. In NAACP Files, 1942
(264:4). A mimeographed script of the "CBS Open Letter on Race Hatred"
is in NAACP Files, 1943 (273:5).

22 As quoted in Lee and Humphrey, *Race Riot*, p. 64.

press for fanning the flames. Negro newsmen and officials of the NAACP quickly replied, and R. J. Thomas added that the police commissioner's statement was "the most serious incitement to race riots that we have seen since the riots themselves."[23]

There was no grand jury investigation. Instead a three-man fact-finding committee, appointed by Governor Kelly and headed by County Prosecutor William E. Dowling, issued a report which blamed the start of the riots on a "group of young Negro hoodlums." The report failed to charge whites who had participated in the violence with any responsibility.[24] Clearly the blame should have been more broadly placed. The underlying tensions made it impossible to find quick solutions to deep-seated problems. Rumors led to violent action on both sides, and there was looting during the riot. The police were unquestionably biased and tended to fire at Negro looters on sight and to ignore whites engaged in acts of violence.[25] A photograph reprinted in *Crisis* (July 1943) incensed Negroes. It showed a policeman holding an injured Negro by both arms while a white rioter struck him in the face. Mayor Jeffries procrastinated in asking Governor Kelly for troops, and Kelly in turn delayed too long before declaring martial law and bringing in the troops. The casualties included not only those killed or injured. The war effort suffered through loss of manpower in nearby war plants, and the cause of democracy at home was injured while the nation was fighting a war for freedom abroad.

The next race riot occurred in New York in August.[26] The incident which set off the New York riot followed a clear pattern

---

23 As quoted in Lee and Humphrey, *Race Riot,* p. 66.

24 As quoted in Lee and Humphrey, *Race Riot,* p. 69. See also Shogan and Craig, *Detroit Race Riot,* pp. 106–7.

25 Alfred Baker Lewis, "Reducing Racial Tensions," *Opportunity* 21 (October 1943): 156. For a highly critical account of the police in Detroit, see Thurgood Marshall, "The Gestapo in Detroit," *Crisis* 50 (August 1943): 232–33, 246–47.

26 Harlem had long been a region for concern. In November 1941, worried about crime in Harlem, the NAACP proposed a conference on the subject and alleged that two earlier reports had been ignored. In NAACP Files, 1943 (275:4). On March 10, 1943, another conference on crime was held in Harlem at the instigation of Walter White. His purpose was to arouse community interest in helping to solve the problem. See "Conference on Harlem Crime. . . . March 10, 1943." In NAACP Files, 1943 (275:4). The concern over crime continued after the riot was over. See "Summary of discussions at meetings on June 9th and 19 regarding Harlem situation" [mimeographed, 2 pp.], June 26, 1944. "Minutes of Confidential Meeting with Mayor La Guardia, June 30, 1944." In NAACP Files, 1944 (291:4). Housing was another matter of concern. See Report of the Sub-Committee on Housing of the City-Wide Citizen's Committee on Harlem, May 1942. In NAACP Files, 1943 (275:4).

—a fight transformed by rumor into unprovoked murder. The rumor spread swiftly through Harlem that a white policeman had shot and killed a Negro soldier without cause. The rumor began when a Negro soldier, his fiancée, and mother returned to the Braddock Hotel, where the mother had stayed while visiting Harlem. When the soldier entered the lobby an intoxicated Negro woman was arguing with a white policeman, and she appealed to bystanders for help. The soldier tried to assist and got into a dispute with the policeman; they began to scuffle. The soldier grabbed the policeman's nightstick and started to run away with it, whereupon the policeman, a rookie, shot the soldier in the shoulder.

The rumor spread that the soldier had been murdered, and the Harlem riot ensued. The day, like that in Detroit earlier in the summer, had been sweltering, and the Negroes in Harlem were increasingly frustrated by reports of police brutality in Detroit, lynchings in the South, unfair treatment of Negroes in the armed forces, and widespread discrimination. Walter White described the riot briefly in a letter to Secretary of War Stimson: "To be understood properly, what took place Sunday night should be divided into two wholly separate time units." The first of these, he noted, "lasting three or four hours, saw the blind, infuriated smashing of store windows on 125th Street for no other reason than that they symbolized a bitterness which had grown among Negroes all over the country." The second time period "began sometime after midnight when looters took advantage of the disorder to pillage."

Mayor La Guardia was on good terms with Negro leaders, and he had appointed A. Philip Randolph as a member of the New York City Housing Authority in April 1942.[27] As soon as he heard of the rioting, La Guardia called Walter White and Roy Wilkins, and by the time they arrived at the West 123rd Street Police Station the mayor had ordered all available police to Harlem and called for military police to get military personnel out of Harlem as soon as possible. At White's suggestion, La Guardia asked for equal numbers of Negro military police to assist in this work. La Guardia, accompanied by White, drove into the riot area and personally tried to disperse a crowd but was persuaded to leave. A sound truck was dispatched through the streets to announce that the Negro soldier had not been killed and to plead for the rioting to cease. The violence was not checked and rioting continued

---

27 *Opportunity* 20 (May 1942): 151.

throughout the night, but the police effectively brought the situation under control by morning.

There were marked differences between the Harlem and Detroit riots. The Harlem riot did not involve a fight between Negroes and whites; rather it was a battle between lower-class Negroes and the police, and apparently it did not matter whether the police were whites or Negroes. There was a question whether this was a race riot in the usual sense of the term.[28] There was no doubt, however, that the riot was the result of Negro frustrations, but Negro leaders neither supported nor condoned it. Lester B. Granger wrote:[29]

> It took race riots in five great cities to wake up white America to the dangers of racial conflict. It took a riot in Harlem to teach Negro America that all racial intolerance is not on one side of the fence and that a Negro riot in action is every bit as bestial and blindly destructive as a white mob.

A writer stated in *Crisis* in January 1945: "The worst situation that a policeman can find himself in is that of having shot a Negro. At such times the fury of the Negro crowds becomes uncontrollable; akin, in spirit, ironically, to a Southern lynch mob."[30]

Rioting Negroes had looted Harlem foodstores and pawnshops in particular and baited the police during the night. A few days later, Mayor La Guardia said, "This is not a race riot. There was no conflict between groups of our citizens. What happened was the thoughtless, criminal acts of hoodlums, reckless, irresponsible people. Shame has come to our city, and sorrow."[31]

A second difference between the riots in Detroit and Harlem was the leadership provided by the mayors. Mayor Jeffries of Detroit was ineffective, while Mayor La Guardia acted quickly and efficiently. Through his example the New York police acted objectively to protect the peace rather than as biased onlookers. The situation also differed in that there were no white participants, aside from those on the police force. Because he took prompt action, Mayor La Guardia did not have to call on state or federal officials for help.

28 For differing views, see Allen D. Grimshaw, ed., *Racial Violence in the United States* (Chicago: Aldine, 1969), pp. 117–19.

29 Lester B. Granger, "Victory Through Unity," *Opportunity* 21 (October 1943): 151.

30 "White Policemen in Harlem," *Crisis* 52 (January 1945): 16.

31 As quoted in *Time* (August 9, 1943): 19.

The third major difference was the lack of a strong "climate of intolerance" among whites in New York.[32] If there was a "religious-political-agitational crowd" in New York, it played no part in the Harlem riot. La Guardia and the Negro leaders enjoyed a strong rapport, and the New York police were not accused of brutality as were the police in Detroit. Adam Clayton Powell, Jr., a New York City councilman, said the police ". . . have proved themselves New York's finest."[33]

The Harlem riot of 1943 was a serious matter—five people died, hundreds were injured, and property damage ran into the millions. Nevertheless, Lee and Humphrey note, Negroes and whites were both proud of the way the riot was handled. There were no residual feelings of guilt and the esprit de corps of Negro and white leaders was enhanced.[34]

Two other disturbances during the summer had less national impact but were noted by Negroes as added reasons for discontent. Violence broke out in the Alabama Dry Dock and Shipbuilding Company of Mobile late in May. White workmen protested against the Negro workers and suddenly, without warning, launched an attack on Negro workmen. Fifty Negroes and one white man were seriously hurt, and 25,000 men stopped work in that vital war industry. The ensuing negotiations produced an unsatisfactory solution—the shipways were segregated and Negroes were allowed to work on hulls but not on the superstructures of the ships under construction. As a result, it was charged, there was a slowdown in construction.[35]

Another disturbance arose in Beaumont, Texas, where it was rumored that a Negro had sexually assaulted the wife of a white serviceman. A white mob reacted to the rumor by attacking, burning, and destroying parts of the Negro section of the city on June 16, 1943. The attack was so sudden that it was over before Negroes could react in force; two Negroes lost their lives, and several were injured. Ironically, a physician who examined the victim of the alleged sexual assault found no evidence of the attack.[36]

---

32 Lee and Humphrey, *Race Riot*, p. 98.

33 As quoted in Lee and Humphrey, *Race Riot*, p. 98.

34 Lee and Humphrey, *Race Riot*, p. 104. For a summary of press reactions to the riots, see *Monthly Summary of Events and Trends in Race Relations* 1:2 (September 1943): 22–25.

35 Thomas, "Race Conflict and Social Action," p. 165. See also Herbert R. Northrup, *Organized Labor and the Negro* (New York: Harper & Brothers, 1944), pp. 226–28.

36 Thomas, "Race Conflict and Social Action," p. 166. See also Shogan and Craig, *Detroit Race Riot*, pp. 7–8.

These episodes of violence were exceptions rather than the rule in the relationships between Negroes and whites during World War II. The records of the war industries and the armed forces indicate that there were strong differences of opinion and vigorous statements made by people of both races; yet violence was not a prevailing mood or mode of action. The white population generally believed that winning the war was a priority and that domestic discord deterred accomplishment of that objective. Negroes, especially the articulate leaders, maintained winning the war as their priority but their war aims were broader. They sought victory for democracy at home as well as abroad and realized that domestic violence weakened the chances for victory on either front. Consequently, they hoped to win the domestic victory by peaceful means. The Negro leaders, with increasing skill, expanded their role in providing national leadership, increased political activity throughout the nation, referred grievances to the courts, and appealed to the sense of justice of all Americans.

CHAPTER 5

Negro during Wartime: The Army and Two Leaders

BEFORE WORLD WAR I, military service was a source of Negro pride. Negro educators, clergymen, and the press frequently referred to Negro heroes of America's past wars. After the Civil War, the army maintained four regular Negro regiments—the 9th and 10th cavalries and the 24th and 25th infantries. These units included veterans of the Civil War and the frontier Indian fighting. Retired sergeants from these organizations often became respected, conservative leaders in their communities.

The Negro tradition of racial and national pride in military service continued during World War I. However, the four historic Negro regiments were not allowed to fight in Europe; they were assigned to continental defense. Most of the 404,348 Negro troops were in the supply services. The 92d and the 93d infantry divisions were formed and shipped to France. The 92d Division was composed mainly of draftees. The division was sent to a "quiet" sector of the French section of the front and briefly moved into an active area from which it was withdrawn shortly thereafter. Near the end of the war in November 1918, the 92d Division joined in an attack on the German line. The 93d Division, comprised of four infantry regiments, was assigned to the French and served on the French sector at the front.

The news reports of Negro action in World War I mostly concerned these two divisions and they differed widely. A United Press report, for example, stated, "American Negroes proved their value as fighters in the line east of Verdun on June 12. . . ."[1] Privates Henry Johnson and Needham Roberts were added to the list of Negro heroes for their exploits in repelling a German raiding party. The press accounts of bravery and accomplishment, however, were accompanied by unsettling rumors and allegations.

---

[1] Quoted in Ulysses Lee, *The Employment of Negro Troops*, The United States Army in World War II: Special Studies (Washington, D.C.: U.S. Government Printing Office, 1966), p. 6. This authoritative source is one of the excellent volumes in the United States Army in World War II series, prepared and published under the aegis of the Office of the Chief of Military History, and based on extensive military files.

There was a report of Negro cowardice and ineptness, and another concerning the mistreatment of Negro soldiers by white officers. Colonel Charles Young, the highest ranking Negro officer, was retired in 1917, and the divisions were staffed by white officers— Negroes were understandably disappointed, and *Crisis* suggested that the army wanted these divisions to fail.

W. E. B. DuBois charged that the policy was to praise the "Negro stevedore and the fighting black private" but "to disparage the black officer and eliminate him from the army despite his record." DuBois published a series of documents in May 1919 to prove his point.[2] DuBois's presentation led Negroes to feel that Negro soldiers and officers performed well given an opportunity and that their failures were the fault of prejudiced white officers. Most Negroes believed that Negro officers and soldiers did not receive full credit for what they had done. These views intensified during the 1920s, especially since the War Department made no effort to clarify the situation.

The War Department conducted a study of the Negro's role in World War I, but it was kept confidential; so the reports were neither widely accepted nor refuted. The studies consisted mostly of reports submitted by white officers under whom Negro troops had served, and their appraisals were generally unflattering to Negroes and especially to Negro officers. The reports reinforced the view that Negro troops should not be assigned to Negro officers and that Negro units would be second rate even with white officers in command. There were other views that took exception to this dismal picture. The commanding officer of the 92d Division, Major General Charles C. Ballou, charged that his division "was made the dumping ground for discards, both white and black."[3] A white officer reported that his men were "generally amenable to discipline, exceedingly uncomplaining under hardship, and the majority willing and ready to follow an officer anywhere and at any time." This officer noted, "Of course there was a large amount of illiteracy, which complicated the non-commissioned officer problem."[4]

The War Department appraisal of the effectiveness of Negro troops in World War I became a guide for the future. Army planners were asked to make recommendations concerning the Negro's role in the army in the event the United States should again

---

2 W. E. B. DuBois, "Documents of the War," *Crisis* 18 (May 1919): 16–21.
3 As quoted in Lee, *Employment of Negro Troops*, p. 18.
4 As quoted in Lee, *Employment of Negro Troops*, p. 19.

be engaged in a major war. However, during the 1920s and early 1930s, army planning was largely theoretical, since appropriations cut the armed forces to a minimum.

The army's planning during this period was an important factor in determining how Negroes were used in World War II. The planning was initially kept secret, and there was little public knowledge of what the army had in mind. The planners dealt with several difficult subjects that arose during World War I— "the use of Negroes as combat troops, the size and nature of Negro units; and the race of officers for Negro units."[5]

The army, about to move into mass mobilization in the summer of 1940, reached the following conclusions about the role of Negroes: Negroes should be enrolled in the army in proportion to their representation in the total population, about 9 percent. They would be used in "both arms and services and in all types of units for which they could qualify."[6] They would serve in all-Negro units and possibly as parts of larger white units. There were differences of opinion concerning the racial mixing of units, but it was agreed the races would be separate within the smaller units. Officers for Negro units could be Negro or white, but Negro officers would be placed in command of only Negro units. Facilities for Negro and white troops were to be of equal quality.

The Negro's concept of his wartime role was partly affected by the tight-lipped response of the War Department to innumerable requests for information. Many Negro leaders consequently believed the army had no plans to use Negroes in the armed forces and began a campaign to ensure there would be a role for the Negro. The *Pittsburgh Courier* began to exert pressure in 1938. Among other things its editorials urged people to send letters to the president and other political leaders. The *Courier* also organized the Committee for Negro Participation in the National Defense. One active campaign called for admitting Negroes into the air corps, and many bills calling for Negro flight training appeared in Congress during the 1930s.[7] The NAACP actively pursued this goal by trying to persuade Congress to pass legislation forcing the army to enroll Negroes in the air corps. An amendment to Public Law 18, effective April 3, 1939, partially achieved

---

5 Lee, *Employment of Negro Troops*, p. 33.

6 Lee, *Employment of Negro Troops*, p. 49.

7 For editorial comments, see *Opportunity* 18 (September 1940): 258; *Crisis* 47 (September 1940): 279. See also James L. H. Peck, "When Do *We* Fly?" *Crisis* 47 (December 1940): 376–78, 388.

the goal by authorizing the secretary of war to lend materials for instruction and training of Negroes to accredited civilian aviation schools, "one or more of which shall be designated by the Civil Aeronautics Administration [CAA] for the training of any Negro air pilot."[8] During the fall of 1939, the CAA established Civilian Pilot Training (CPT) units at a number of Negro colleges, including Tuskegee, Hampton, and Howard. Negro leaders were unsatisfied and continued to press for full acceptance of Negroes into the air corps. Unknown to the public, there was strong opposition within the air corps, where it was argued that separate Negro units were not feasible. Further, the abilities of Negro officers were questioned, as though they were not suited to the hazards of flying. The air corps gave no indication of admitting Negroes, and the pressure from Negroes continued. A typical caption under a photograph of planes on an assembly line read, "Warplanes— Negro Americans may not build them, repair them, or fly them, but they must help pay for them."[9]

It was not announced, but the army developed a policy in 1939 which would include some Negroes in the air corps. The plan envisaged training Negro pilots and mechanics in single-seat-pursuit and observation planes. The training of enlisted men to service the planes would require several years. The plan began operating in 1941.

Negro leaders warned that even if Negroes were admitted to the armed forces they might be used solely in subordinate roles. William H. Hastie asserted:[10]

> We will be American soldiers. We will be American ditchdiggers. We will be American laborers. We will be anything that any other American should be in this whole program of national defense. But we won't be black auxiliaries.

The Selective Service and Training Act of 1940 initially proposed that "in a free society the obligations and privileges of military training and service should be shared generally in accordance with a fair and just system of selective compulsory military training and service." This vague statement failed to satisfy Negro leaders, and they lobbied for a more definite statement. The act stated that under a quota determined

---

[8] As quoted in Lee, *Employment of Negro Troops,* pp. 56–57.
[9] *Crisis* 47 (July 1940), cover photograph.
[10] As quoted in Lee, *Employment of Negro Troops,* p. 68.

for the subdivision in which he resides, any person, regardless of race or color, between the ages of eighteen and thirty-six, shall be afforded an opportunity to volunteer for induction into the land or naval forces of the United States for the training and service prescribed.

A second section prescribed "that in the selection and training of men under this act, there shall be no discrimination against any person on account of race or color." The provision of another section disturbed some Negro leaders, since it provided that no man would be accepted for induction and training "unless and until he is acceptable to the land or naval forces for such training and service and his physical and mental fitness for such training has been satisfactorily determined." Negroes feared that "acceptability" would be defined so as to exclude them from military service and that "unless and until" might be used to delay or even prevent their induction.

Accordingly, several Negro leaders—Walter White, T. Arnold Hill, and A. Philip Randolph—drafted a memorandum and presented it to President Roosevelt in the White House conference of September 27, 1940. The memorandum raised several important questions relating to the integration of the Negro into the armed services. It recommended full use of Negro reserve officers and the training of additional officers. It asked for an immediate and broad expansion of centers to train Negroes in the air corps and argued that, in addition to Negro pilots, provision should be made for training Negroes as bombardiers, gunners, radiomen, and navigators. The delegation also urged that all other units of the army accept Negroes and that specialized personnel "such as Negro physicians, dentists, pharmacists" be admitted. In addition, the group called for techniques "for insuring the policy of integration in the Navy other than the menial services to which Negroes are now restricted." The delegation concluded with a request for the introduction of trained Negro women as nurses into the army and navy as well as the Red Cross.[11]

The administration had already moved in some of the directions urged by the delegation. The White House ordered the army to prepare for release a statement that "colored men will have equal opportunity with white men in all departments of the Army."[12]

[11] Walter White, *A Man Called White: The Autobiography of Walter White* (New York: Viking Press, 1948), pp. 186–87. See also *Crisis* 47 (November 1940).

[12] As quoted in Lee, *Employment of Negro Troops*, p. 75.

In a Cabinet meeting on September 13, President Roosevelt expressed a similar view. The Selective Service and Training Act was approved on September 16, and the War Department reported that 36,000 of the first 400,000 men called would be Negroes.

On October 8, 1940, Assistant Secretary of War Robert P. Patterson submitted a statement to the president which had been approved by the secretary of war, "as a result of a conference in your office on September 27." The statement was approved by Roosevelt and released to the press on October 9. The document included the following provisions:

1. The number of Negroes in the army would be "maintained on the general basis of the proportion of the Negro population of the country."
2. Negro organizations would be established in "each major branch of the service, combatant as well as noncombatant."
3. Negro reserve officers eligible for active duty would be "assigned to Negro units officered by colored personnel."
4. "When officer candidate schools are established, opportunity will be given to Negroes to qualify for reserve commissions."
5. "Negroes are being given aviation training as pilots, mechanics and technical specialists. This training will be accelerated."
6. Negro civilians who were qualified would be given positions in arsenals and army posts.
7. "The policy of the War Department is not to intermingle colored and white enlisted personnel in the same regimental organization."

This lengthy statement went on to report that the system worked well and that morale was high.[13]

The White House implied that this policy statement was supported by the Negro delegation, and the result was a storm of protest. The members of the delegation felt they had been misled,[14] and other Negro leaders who thought the delegates had approved the statement accused them of selling out. Negroes particularly objected to part 5 for not promising to extend Negro enlistments into other categories in the air corps and to part 7 because it reiterated the policy of segregation to which many Negroes objected. Despite protests by Negroes, the army accepted the statement as a directive from the commander in chief. The document, however, "helped clinch the belief, held by most Negroes, that there was a

---

13 Cited in Lee, *Employment of Negro Troops,* pp. 75–76.
14 White, *A Man Called White,* p. 187.

wide gap between the words and the intentions of the War Department."[15]

Several actions helped lessen the ill will resulting from the White House policy statement. The War Department announced that new units would be formed and that Negroes would be segregated but that they would serve in all branches and services. Then, on October 25, Colonel Benjamin O. Davis, senior Negro army officer, was nominated for promotion to brigadier general. The nomination was later approved by the Senate. In addition, Secretary of War Stimson announced the appointment of Hastie as his civilian aide on Negro affairs on October 25. Hastie took office on November 1 and was instructed to help the army plan the organization of Negro units and to investigate complaints regarding the treatment of Negro military and civilian personnel in the War Department. He was also to "cooperate with the Negro representatives on the Selective Service Committee and in the Labor Section of the Advisory Commission to the Council of National Defense where appropriate."[16] Hastie's appointment was a victory for the Negro leadership, which had lobbied so hard in Washington.

During the war, army officials assumed that the president's statement was the national policy and they refused to debate the segregation issue. Army historian Ulysses Lee said the army's task "was not to alter American social customs but to create a fighting machine with a maximum economy of time and effort."[17] *Crisis* and other voices of Negro opinion, however, continued to hammer away against segregation. In addition, they tried to improve the status of Negro soldiers within the segregated system. They carefully watched the army's performance against the yardstick of the president's policy statement and quickly drew attention to any deviation. Two main criticisms appeared: charges that Negroes were mistreated and an often expressed fear that Negro soldiers would not be used in combat.

A study of the advances made toward equality and the role of Negro leadership during World War II should include a brief examination of the part played by Hastie in the War Department. His first important move came in September 1941, after ten months of "observation, discussion, and action in the War Depart-

---

[15] Lee, *Employment of Negro Troops*, p. 77.
[16] As quoted in Lee, *Employment of Negro Troops*, p. 80.
[17] Lee, *Employment of Negro Troops*, p. 83.

ment and in the field."[18] His recommendations came while the army was rapidly expanding and the nation was still at peace. He contended that more Negroes could be used in the army and that they could be used more effectively. Drawing attention to "the fundamental error of philosophy and approach," he charged: "The traditional mores of the South have been widely accepted and adopted by the Army as the basis of policy and practice affecting the Negro soldier." Thus Negro and white soldiers were separated as far as possible.

Hastie noted that only about 5 percent of the army was Negro as opposed to the 9 percent figure announced as a base and that Negroes were being "disproportionately concentrated in the Corps of Engineers, the Quartermaster Corps, and Overhead installations." Hastie challenged the claim that the assignment of large numbers of Negroes to labor functions was justified by their illiteracy; he noted that illiterates were no longer accepted and that the evidence indicated that a high percentage of men with little education or skill at the time of their induction could be effective in combat units.

Hastie's criticisms were followed by the positive recommendation that new organizations should be established as soon as possible to accommodate Negro selectees, that the combat regiments should be made part of larger units, and that isolated small units of Negroes should be transferred to eliminate the need for separate recreational facilities. Hastie's final recommendation was fundamental—he suggested that a start should be made in using soldiers without racial separation.

Hastie submitted his memorandum through Under Secretary Patterson, who forwarded it to General Marshall with a request that Marshall consider it carefully and preferably discuss it with him. Two and one-half months later Patterson discussed the matter with Major General William Bryden, Marshall's deputy chief of staff.

No one seriously questioned Hastie's first points, but the recommendation that segregation be stopped was controversial. Hastie believed a move away from segregation should start while the nation was at peace, since he realized it might be difficult to make such a start once we were in the war. He further believed the experiment would stimulate high morale. The delay in considering the memorandum damaged the proposal. Unfortunately, the general staff thought that Hastie had recommended a social revolution in time of war. General Marshall wrote a commentary on the

---

[18] Cited in Lee, *Employment of Negro Troops,* pp. 136–39.

Hastie memorandum to the secretary of war on December 1. The general asserted that Hastie's solution[19]

> would be tantamount to solving a social problem that has perplexed the American people throughout the history of this nation. The Army cannot accomplish such a solution, and should not be charged with the undertaking. The settlement of vexing racial problems cannot be permitted to complicate the tremendous task of the War Department and thereby jeopardize discipline and morale.

Thus, even before Pearl Harbor, Hastie and the War Department were deadlocked on the issue.

Meanwhile, Hastie was acting as a liaison with the Negro public. He and the War Department's public information bureau scheduled a conference with Negro editors and publishers on December 8, obviously with no foreknowledge of the Pearl Harbor attack December 7. General Marshall detailed the actions of the army so far in distributing Negro soldiers in "all our arms and services" and in training, and stated that he was not satisfied with the progress made to date. He then publicly announced that a Negro division was being considered. The generally good impression made by General Marshall's speech was shattered an hour later when Colonel Eugene R. Householder from the adjutant general's office made a statement on the question of segregation. He announced that the army did not create the problem, that the army consisted of people with individual views, and that army orders could not change these views. The army, he continued, would not be "made the means of engendering conflict among the mass of people because of a stand with respect to Negroes which is not compatible with the position attained by the Negro in civilian life." He declared, "The Army is not a sociological laboratory."[20]

Most editors of Negro publications were shocked by this statement, but they rationalized—they counted more on Marshall's vaguely expressed interest in change than on the statement of his junior officer. Nevertheless, the colonel's statement limited the success of the conference. Walter White wrote to General Marshall several weeks later and used the general's expressed dissatisfaction with current progress as an opening to recommending the creation

---

19 Cited in Lee, *Employment of Negro Troops,* pp. 140–41.

20 Cited in Lee, *Employment of Negro Troops,* p. 142. For an example of War Department publicity, see War Department, Bureau of Public Relations Press Branch, January 22, 1942: "Army Announces Plans to Form 93rd Infantry Division and 100th Pursuit Squadron." In NAACP Files, 1944 (264:2).

of a volunteer division "open to all irrespective of race, creed, color or national origin." White followed with another letter changing the recommendation from "division" to "regiment." He received what he considered to be a form letter in response, and White concluded that the army did not intend to change its policy toward the Negro despite the public statements. The lieutenant colonel who had forwarded the alleged form letter to White defended his action vigorously. He praised Hastie as a person but asserted that the War Department was confronted with a "condition that bids fair to be cancerous." He charged that Hastie considered himself "a representative of the National Association for the Advancement of Colored People first, and a representative of the War Department second." He wrote that his letter to White might have been "curt" but that White's letters to the War Department had been "increasingly insolent on subjects which are of no concern to the National Association for the Advancement of Colored People."[21]

Since these views were apparently shared by many officials in the War Department, there is some question as to whether Hastie was successful in his effort to change the War Department. The immediate result was a setback, since Hastie failed to change the policy of segregation, and he soon found that he was no longer consulted on many matters relating to the Negro. Hastie continued his work, however, and made some headway in implementing his recommendations. He met with Secretary Stimson and Under Secretary Patterson on January 13, 1942, and pressed for the transfer of small Negro units and for the creation of new air force units. He repeated his recommendation for a start toward integration but received no encouragement. Hastie became increasingly convinced that the army was not doing all it could for the Negro.

The Advisory Committee on Negro Troop Policies was formed on August 27, 1942, headed by Assistant Secretary of War John J. McCloy. Hastie's lack of influence was underscored, since he was neither appointed as a member nor informed of the committee's existence. He learned of it informally a month after it had been established. He was naturally distressed and wished to resign, but Patterson persuaded him to remain at his post by assuring him that he was useful.

Hastie was also becoming more and more concerned over developments in the air forces. A separate air corps flying school

---

21 Cited in Lee, *Employment of Negro Troops,* pp. 143–45. White does not refer to this incident in his memoirs.

was established at Tuskegee, and the NAACP and some of the Negro press bitterly opposed it as Jim Crowism. They dubbed the Negro pilots trained there "Lonely Eagles." The air corps felt it had to move slowly in adding Negroes in order to give the first pursuit squadron a chance to prove itself, but Negro critics charged that the air corps had placed undue restrictions on the use of Negroes. Hastie agreed that the air corps was not meeting its commitments, and he kept asking questions which annoyed some of the air corps leaders.

The Technical Training Command presented a plan in October which called for completely separate training of Negroes in the air forces at Tuskegee and at Jefferson Barracks in St. Louis. Supporters of the proposal felt that locating a training center in St. Louis, near a large civilian population of Negroes, would act as a safeguard against discrimination. Hastie was not consulted at any time nor was he told of the discussions. When he heard rumors in November that Jefferson Barracks would be converted into an all-Negro training center, he asked Assistant Secretary of War for Air Robert A. Lovett for confirmation. The reply he received three weeks later did not mention the plans for Jefferson Barracks. When, on January 1, 1943, it was announced at Jefferson Barracks that a new officer candidate school for Negroes would open on January 15, Hastie felt that his usefulness to the War Department had come to an end. He notified Secretary Stimson and Under Secretary Patterson that in the air forces "further retrogression is now so apparent and recent occurrences are so objectionable and inexcusable that I have no alternative but to resign in protest and to give public expression to my views."[22] He made no statement until his resignation became effective at the end of the month, and he asked his two assistants, Louis Lautier and Truman K. Gibson, Jr., to remain at their posts. In his public statement after leaving office, he criticized the War Department for misleading statements and raised objections to some of its policies. The War Department studied his statement, denied the factual validity of some of his allegations, and moved to correct some of the examples of discrimination to which he had drawn attention.

Certainly, from the short-range point of view of accomplishing his immediate objectives, Hastie had lost. His forthright and aggressive ways had weakened his usefulness in the eyes of many leaders in the War Department and had so reduced his influence with them that they ignored or avoided him. Undoubtedly, Hastie

---

22 Memo quoted in Lee, *Employment of Negro Troops*, p. 171.

took the only course of action open to him, and as soon as he saw that he could not accomplish his objectives within the War Department, he left to be free to criticize its actions in public speeches and writings. Whether Hastie could have accomplished more for the cause of integration in the army by being less aggressive and remaining within the department is a subject for conjecture.

The career of Benjamin O. Davis, the first Negro brigadier general, is also worthy of comment. A member of the inspector general's office, General Davis was appointed to the McCloy advisory committee, to which Hastie had not been appointed. Unlike Hastie, Davis could not readily resign and he had to work within the organization. General Davis prepared a proposal for the operation of the advisory committee which suggested that it recommend "the breaking down of the so-called 'Jim Crow' practices within the War Department and on the military reservations, and the securing of the cooperation of the communities near the reservations to that end."[23] He made several other proposals including the establishment of orientation courses to acquaint white soldiers with the contributions of Negroes. Davis also tried to eliminate the use of terms derogatory to Negroes. His suggestions were not acted on immediately, but they bore fruit later. Throughout the war, General Davis acted as a kind of troubleshooter, sometimes reporting on racial incidents and sometimes attempting to raise the esteem of Negro troops in the eyes of the War Department. The advisory committee was continued, and General Davis proved to be an important part of it and also a valuable member of the inspector general's staff.

The cases of Hastie and Davis are not cited here to either disparage or praise one compared to the other. Each worked to improve the status of the Negro in the armed forces. Hastie's direct impact on the War Department while he was in office was probably minimal because of the opposition he aroused by urging a move away from segregation. His real effectiveness came from the outside, and his resignation prompted the War Department to take action which it had avoided to that date. Hastie became a symbol of the Negro's dissatisfaction with the army's reluctance to change its attitudes. Davis symbolized the Negro who had made good in the army. His work, alluded to briefly, was probably little known outside the War Department. Hastie and Davis repeated the old story of one man fighting against segregation and the other against discrimination.

---

[23] Cited in Lee, *Employment of Negro Troops*, p. 160.

CHAPTER 6

Negro in Uniform: Enlistment and Training

THE ENLISTMENT AND SERVICE of Negroes in the army during World War II involved many problems.[1] First, the rate of acceptance for induction of Negroes was lower than the rate for whites. For example, 30.3 percent of eligible whites and 46 percent of eligible Negroes had been rejected by the end of 1943. Negro rejections were mainly attributed to venereal disease and failure to meet the minimum educational requirements. The development and widespread use of sulfa drugs largely solved the first problem, but the inadequate education of Negro inductees was a problem more difficult to solve. The rejections seriously limited the service Negroes could contribute to the army and its operations, and many who were accepted barely met the minimum requirements.

After induction, selectees were tested and interviewed before being classified for service. The main test, the Army General Classification Test (AGCT), was used to sort soldiers according to their ability to learn. Many observers regarded the AGCT as an intelligence test but it was not. The army chief psychologist explained: "It does not measure merely inherent mental capacity. Performance in such a test reflects very definitely the educational opportunities the individual has had and the way in which these opportunities have been grasped and utilized." He elaborated: "There is nothing in the title of the Army test that says anything about native intelligence. It is a classification test. Its purpose is to classify soldiers into categories according to how ready they are to pick up soldiering."[2] The test was disadvantageous for Negroes who had entered the army with serious educational deficiencies, from poor or inadequate schools, and who had no experience

---

[1] In this chapter, as in the past one, for factual information I have relied on Ulysses Lee, *The Employment of Negro Troops*, The United States Army in World War II: Special Studies (Washington, D.C.: U.S. Government Printing Office, 1966).

[2] Dr. Walter V. Bingham, Chief Psychologist, Classification and Replacement Branch, Adjutant General's Office, as cited in Lee, *Employment of Negro Troops*, p. 242. On the AGCT, see Robert R. Palmer, Bell I. Wiley, and William R. Keast, *The Procurement and Training of Ground Combat Troops*, The United States Army in World War II: The Army Ground Forces (Washington, D.C.: U.S. Government Printing Office, 1948), p. 6.

with extracurricular activities involving playgrounds, newspapers, radios, and movies.

The army was interested in the "working ability" and promise of quick development of inductees and accordingly separated those tested with AGCT into Grades I to V. The army officials expected that Grades I, II, and III would produce leaders, enlisted specialists, and technicians. Grades IV and V categorized semiskilled soldiers and laborers. It was found that Negroes and whites of comparable background and education did equally well on the tests; others did poorly. A mechanical aptitude test was also administered to inductees, and the disparity of performance between whites and most Negroes was greater in this test.

The army's major problem with the high percentage of low-scoring Negroes was in placing them. Similar numbers of low-scoring whites were easier to absorb, since they were proportionately fewer. Units in which up to 50 percent of the trainees were from Grade V, as was the case in some Negro units, could expect overall performance to be adversely affected. The difficulty of distributing Grade V trainees widely was compounded, since many units strongly opposed infusions of "low intelligence" Negroes. The air corps found it easier to screen out low-scoring soldiers by emphasizing the technical aspects of its operations.

The army completed several studies in an effort to cope with the problem, and in April 1943 the McCloy Advisory Committee submitted a revised plan. The plan proposed a new induction screening process and the establishment of special training units for Grade V inductees who showed the greatest potential. Non-language tests for illiterates and non-English-speaking inductees were introduced, and the plan went into operation in June 1943. The adjutant general reported it to be a success, and 10.6 percent of the Negroes in Grade V were retained.

The physical fitness of soldiers was essential to the strength of the army, and it was found that Negroes had a significantly higher incidence of venereal disease.[3] The army changed its policy and admitted those who had been cured of venereal disease, and it thereafter had to maintain prophylactic programs to prevent reinfection and spread of disease. The generally low literacy rate and socioeconomic level of many Negroes inhibited their under-

---

[3] Lee, *Employment of Negro Troops*, pp. 240, 276–90. See also Louis Lautier, "Sidelights on the Negro and the Army," *Opportunity* 22 (January–March 1944): 7–8.

standing and acceptance of prophylactic measures and made the problem time-consuming. It was particularly acute where large concentrations of Negro soldiers were assigned. At Fort Huachuca in Arizona the army tried to cope with the problem by regulating a red-light district, declaring the area off limits, and ordering prophylactic treatment for everyone who went off the post. At Tuskegee, Alabama, the vigorous program of "subvenereal disease control" included assigning noncommissioned officers to work with small groups to educate and motivate individuals. The program reduced the rate of infection so successfully that it was adopted elsewhere.

The army was also concerned with troop morale and so were Hastie and Negro pressure groups which were keeping an eye on their men in uniform. Negroes experienced all the customary problems affecting the morale of newly uniformed civilians, as well as problems unique to Negroes. They were frequently shifted from one post to another and, each time, had the uncomfortable task of discovering what their status was to be. The routine needs for transportation, getting haircuts, and using a gym or a bowling alley were all affected by the attitudes of nearby communities. The northern Negro recently arrived in a southern army camp found these problems to be critical.

The NAACP was soon the recipient of requests for aid to Negro servicemen. The pleas came to branch offices and directly to national headquarters from friends, relatives, and the soldiers themselves. The NAACP Legal Defense Division responded conscientiously and in time developed guidelines to handle the large number and variety of requests. One staff member explained, "Our rules prohibit us from handling cases other than those involving: (1) discrimination against the Negro, (2) denial of the civil rights to the Negro in general, and (3) where the person concerned is destitute and innocent."[4] Another staff member wrote, "The only time the Association enters a case is when it appears that the case may be of national importance to the Negro race." He added, "We are not equipped to handle every case involving a Negro or even every case involving Negro soldiers."[5]

The NAACP declined to handle purely military cases saying, in one instance, there is "nothing we can do for a man who had

---

[4] Edward R. Dudley, Assistant Special Counsel, to Mrs. Green, July 10, 1944. In NAACP Files, 1944 (283:2).

[5] Milton R. Konvitz, Assistant Special Counsel, to Oscar Dennis, June 5, 1944. In NAACP Files, 1944 (283:2).

been AWOL 6 times."[6] Other reasons included a "matter of principle," when "the party is guilty of the alleged crime,"[7] and a
belief that "the right Negro [had been] charged, tried, found
guilty and properly sentenced—and had had his day in court."[8]
The national office did not reach the last conclusion solely on the
basis of a letter; it checked into the case before deciding not to
intervene.

The legal staff naturally wished to be sure of its position in each
case and usually sought strong evidence in advance. Hastie agreed:
"I am reluctant to accuse an officer of an extremely serious crime
without some indication that the charge can be substantiated."[9]
When the staff decided to investigate a case, it normally discussed
the matter by letter or in person with Hastie or with his successor,
Truman K. Gibson, Jr. General Davis sometimes went to the loca-
tion in question to investigate the problem. In one such case a
man was restored to full military duty with no loss of pay.[10] Another case involved a Negro soldier sentenced to twenty-five years
imprisonment for participating in a "riotous assembly" at March
Field in California. The riotous assembly arose because Negroes
were banned from the base theater and service clubs. The NAACP
Legal Defense Division subsequently asserted: "It is our considered opinion that the Army High Command cannot continue to
ignore the fact that soldiers called upon to sacrifice and die for
democracy will bitterly resent the practice of segregation and discrimination by the Army itself." The defense contended that the
soldier's arrest "flowed naturally, logically, and spontaneously
from the race policy in force there" and, although the sentence
had already been reduced to twenty years, urged the case be "re-
examined with the view of clemency."[11]

The hostility of civilian police toward Negro soldiers especially
disturbed the NAACP. A member of the legal staff wrote that despite the War Department's assertion that it lacked jurisdiction in

---

[6] Handwritten note signed TM. In NAACP Files, 1942 (264:3). See also
another letter in the same folder, Thurgood Marshall to Malcolm D. Hall,
June 29, 1944.

[7] Edward R. Dudley to Sidney R. Redmond, St. Louis Branch, NAACP,
May 11, 1944. In NAACP Files, 1944 (283:2).

[8] See comments on letter Local Board NAACP (Shreveport, La.) to NAACP
(New York), January 13, 1942. In NAACP Files, 1942 (264:3).

[9] William H. Hastie [signed Bill] to Frank Reeves, March 21, 1942. In
NAACP Files, 1942 (264:3).

[10] Edward R. Dudley to W. B. Black, January 7, 1944; Black to Dudley,
January 12, 1944. In NAACP Files, 1944 (283:2).

[11] Letter, Administrative Assistant to Henry L. Stimson, Secretary of War,
December 9, 1943. In NAACP Files, 1944 (283:3).

such cases, "we have not hesitated to point out to them that it is their responsibility to protect soldiers under their command particularly when the soldier is subject to the authority of the various armed services." He enclosed a handbook the department had prepared to govern the handling of these cases and recommended:[12]

> In cases where colored soldiers have been brutally mistreated by local police officers, the facts should be called to the attention of the Governors of the various states requesting that they investigate and submit the same to the Grand Jury.

The NAACP issued national press releases in serious cases. The Legal Defense Division and the civilian aide to the secretary of war agreed on most issues. Once in a while the civilian aide, because of his closer association with the army and its problems, was more pragmatic. In July 1942, for example, Walter White received a news clipping which indicated that the people of Eagle Pass, Texas, protested Negro soldiers being sent to their area. White sent the following message to Hastie: "I am sure we do not need to urge you to do what you can to see that the War Department resist any attempt on the part of the prejudiced Texans to try to run the War Department." Hastie replied, "However, the situation is not so simple as it might first appear. I understand that there is only one Negro family in Eagle Pass and there is no Negro community anywhere in the vicinity." Hastie's view, therefore, was that "it really seems to be a bad place to station these men," and he gloomily concluded, "however, the military authorities have felt that in this and many other cases military considerations outweigh the convenience either of the civilian population or the soldiers who will be immediately affected."[13]

When Hastie inquired into troop morale, he was referred to the morale division in the adjutant general's office, which was concerned simply with recreational, library, and other facilities. Hastie learned that morale was a function of command and the responsibility of commanding officers. The quality of leadership, therefore, greatly affected morale and that quality varied from post to post. The morale division's goal was to provide equal

---

[12] Edward R. Dudley to Rev. L. A. Bland, April 20, 1944. In NAACP Files, 1944 (283:3).

[13] Walter White to William H. Hastie, July 13, 1942; Hastie to White, July 15, 1942. In NAACP Files, 1942 (264:3).

facilities for all, but unfortunately the rapid expansion of troop facilities made it impossible to keep pace with the demand. The practice of maintaining separate facilities for the races at first complemented the army policy of racially segregating its units.[14]

During the war the policy toward one type of recreation changed. At first, separation was rigidly maintained and many Negroes became quite dissatisfied. Their athletic facilities were relatively poor, and since they were not allowed to compete against whites, they often could not find teams to play or they had to play teams from nearby Negro high schools or colleges, sometimes from penitentiaries. Later, some posts began admitting Negroes to their athletic teams in football, baseball, and boxing and the Negroes' morale improved noticeably. Heavyweight champion Sergeant Joe Louis completed an exhibition tour of army posts in 1943 and 1944 which was a real stimulus to goodwill.[15]

Entertainment was either a benefit or an irritant. Traveling road shows at some bases performed in post theaters for whites and in segregated mess halls for Negroes. Singer Lena Horne was so annoyed at restrictions placed on members of her race at one post that she gave a separate performance in the Negro USO of a nearby town.[16] In March 1943 the army prohibited the designation of recreational facilities by race. The words "White" and "Colored" were replaced with such designations as "No. 1" and "No. 2." More important, the policy abolished the practice of creating separate facilities. Thereafter, Negroes were allowed to use the same facilities as white soldiers but at different times.

The army had the authority to issue directives to regulate conduct on its own posts, but it did not have authority over the surrounding communities. Most army posts were located in the South and Southwest, where the communities traditionally maintained rules and customs governing relationships between the races. In the North, aside from posts near large cities, the surrounding communities had few if any civilian Negroes and even fewer facilities available to Negro soldiers. Morale problems frequently arose when Negro soldiers lacked recreational facilities or when adjacent communities had few Negroes.

---

14 Following are a few of the many types of protest against racial segregation for troops: "Urban League Executive Deplores Army's Policy of Racial Segregation for Troops," National Urban League Publicity Service, New York, October 16, 1940. In National Urban League Files, Series VI, Box 13. NAACP Board of Directors opposes separate Negro division in Army, NAACP Board of Directors Minutes, January 5, 1942, p. 6. In NAACP Files, Series A, Box 11.
15 Lee, *Employment of Negro Troops*, p. 307.
16 Lee, *Employment of Negro Troops*, pp. 307–8.

Transportation presented a continuing problem. Army officials could not order local bus companies in the South to abolish Jim Crow practices. More than one commander solved the problem by establishing post-operated bus systems on a nonsegregated basis. In terms of railroad travel, Hastie campaigned for the elimination of Jim Crow. His main argument was based on a Supreme Court decision made in April 1941 *(Mitchell v. U.S. et al.)*. This decision stated that Negroes who bought first-class tickets had to be provided accommodations equal in comfort and convenience to those provided whites. The Judge Advocate General's Office supported the right of sergeants to first-class accommodations until the office reversed the policy in a case arising in Virginia involving four Negro second lieutenants who refused to move to a Negro coach. The Judge Advocate General's Office held this to be a case of segregation rather than discrimination, since the coaches were of comparable quality. The Judge Advocate General ruled that the railroad had therefore fulfilled its obligation. Hastie vigorously opposed that position and asserted that the Virginia State Segregation Law did not apply in interstate commerce. Office representatives admitted that Hastie had a point, but said that the army would abide by state legislation until a ruling was made by a higher court.[17] Wartime travel was usually so congested that racial incidents often arose. Fortunately, none erupted into major violence.

Hastie and General Davis both urged the army to attempt to reduce racial friction by fiat. A directive issued in February 1942 reminded post commanders of army regulations designed to improve morale. Superiors were ordered not to "injure those under their authority by tyrannical or capricious conduct or by abusive language." It was pointed out: "In this connection the use of any epithet deemed insulting to a racial group should be carefully avoided. Similarly, commanders should avoid all practices tending to give the colored soldier cause to feel that the Army makes any differentiation between him and any other soldier." Local post commanders often issued directives along the same lines. Sometimes the admonitions were general; sometimes they were direct, especially with regard to the use of epithets toward the Negro. These efforts were well meaning, but they did not eliminate the feeling among Negroes that restrictions they had endured as civilians had followed them into the armed services. Negro sensitivity thus increased.

---

[17] Lee, *Employment of Negro Troops*, pp. 316–20.

Military leadership was undoubtedly essential to troop morale, and, more important, it was an essential ingredient of a successful fighting force. Leadership of Negro troops was a problem of particular concern. Throughout the war the army struggled to set standards for the right kinds of officers. The standards tended to make it impossible to find enough qualified officers. Brigadier General Horace L. Whitaker summarized the problem by stating that the three fundamentals of leadership were even more important in handling Negro troops. "The only difference," he said, "was in the importance of each." The most important aspect of leadership with white troops was "knowing your work. . . . With colored troops it is the least important. The reaction of colored troops makes it more important that their officers convince them that they are getting a square deal. It is next to most important that they be convinced that their officer is interested in them."[18]

Negro and white officers shared problems of leadership. There were never enough Negro officers; in 1940, there were five in the regular army and three of them were chaplains. Most Negro officers were in the reserve corps. The army was still trying to decide which of five proposed plans to follow for the use of Negro officers, and on November 9, 1940, it was decided to employ Negro officers as follows: they would be called to active duty "in the same proportion to the total number of eligible negro [sic] Reserve officers, as the number of white Reserve officers."[19] They would be assigned to fill the complements of the three Negro national guard regiments, and the rest would be used to fill the officer complements of a Negro regiment to be organized later. Unfortunately, those in charge were more concerned with filling vacancies than with developing leadership, and all but one of the four all-Negro regiments had command problems from the start. Hastie helped prompt the army to increase the training of new Negro officers but that attempt started very slowly. The move to increase the number of Negro officers was accompanied by statistics which showed that there was an inadequate number of Negroes in the army who could qualify, "enough," one ground forces officer estimated, "to meet 10% of the total requirements for colored units."[20] The problem was ironically compounded because some units were understaffed with Negro officers and other units overstaffed due to a system of mass transfers. Some units objected to

---

18 As quoted in Lee, *Employment of Negro Troops*, p. 191.
19 Cited in Lee, *Employment of Negro Troops*, p. 195.
20 As quoted in Lee, *Employment of Negro Troops*, p. 211.

the assignment of Negro officers, and other units indicated they did not have separate facilities. Southern communities, supported by their congressmen, tried to prevent the assignment of Negro officers in their areas.

Negro officers were also inhibited by the World War I stereotype and a resulting lack of confidence in their abilities. High-ranking white officers charged that Negro officers lacked proficiency. Lieutenant General Ben Lear, commanding the Second Army, for example, asked that no officers of the rank of major or higher be assigned to staff Negro units. The assignment of white and Negro officers to the same units did not work out well, and yet segregation prevented the development of esprit de corps. White officers were treated preferentially in the assignment of duties, and Negro officers often felt as if they were "extras." White officers assigned to Negro units were frequently unhappy; they were often looked down on by other white officers. Even when they were conscientious, their tasks were often more difficult and time-consuming. The army tried to alleviate the situation by rotating officers. The rotation policy was welcomed by white officers but was of no help to Negro officers, since there was no place for them to go.

The army was a poor training ground for developing Negro leadership. Too many Negroes in the army were handicapped by poor educational and socioeconomic backgrounds and could not qualify as officers. Too many Negroes who were commissioned were frustrated by the system and had neither an opportunity nor the motivation to develop leadership qualities.

The introduction of large numbers of Negro soldiers into new surroundings throughout the country resulted in what Ulysses Lee has called a "harvest of disorders." He noted that there were many racial disturbances but that "the actual rate of serious, generalized outbreaks of racial violence involving Negro troops in World War II was small."[21]

Nevertheless, the possibility remained that any incident might provoke a widespread riot. Most of the training camps were in the South, where the fears of Negroes and whites were easily expanded by rumors and embellishment of even trivial incidents. The disturbances involved Negro and white soldiers, military policemen, city policemen, and civilians in varying degrees. The spring and summer of 1941 brought the first infusions of large numbers of Negro soldiers to the South and there were several

---

21 Lee, *Employment of Negro Troops*, p. 348.

disquieting incidents. One of the first occurred in Georgia, where a Negro soldier was found hanged with his hands tied behind his back in a wooded part of Fort Benning. Negroes believed it was a lynching that proved Negroes in uniform were not immune. Whites believed it a suicide despite the evidence. Tensions understandably rose, and a fight started between white Civilian Conservation Corps (CCC) workers and Negro soldiers over the use of a recreational facility in South Carolina. The friction spread to nearby Columbia and for the next few months minor clashes recurred between Negro soldiers and the military police.

Barroom brawls, excessive drinking, and verbal abuse frequently expanded into more general disturbances. One such episode nearly erupted into major violence in Tampa, Florida. Quarrels over bus transportation caused other incidents and in Fayetteville, North Carolina, a city policeman shot a Negro sergeant. A particularly intense encounter involving Negro soldiers from Chicago and Detroit, military police, townspeople, and state police occurred in Gurdon, Arkansas. A few white officers tried to protect their Negro troops and were attacked. In fear of attacks by the local citizenry and police, several Negro soldiers left the area and returned to their former post in Michigan. The morale of that battalion was low for months thereafter.

Army officials introduced countermeasures to minimize recurrence of racial disturbances, and they tried to upgrade and improve the training of military police. Hastie sought to resolve some of the problems by urging the use of discussion groups composed of whites and Negroes to reach "better understanding and more wholesome relationships."[22] Toward the end of 1941, the War Department created a Special Service Branch, formed to solve problems of military-civilian disorders and white-Negro relationships. Hastie urged this body and the public information bureau to conduct a publicity campaign to improve the situation and in the late spring of 1942, a special report stated, "Bi-racial incidents in the Army are not premeditated and most of them could have been avoided through proper education, leadership and discipline."[23]

The disturbances had an adverse effect on public opinion, and the Negro press and Negro leaders noted that there was a disparity between what was happening to Negro soldiers and the announced war aims of the nation. After one of the disturbances, a

22 As quoted in Lee, *Employment of Negro Troops,* p. 359.
23 Quoted in Lee, *Employment of Negro Troops,* p. 362.

white Richmond, Virginia, editor wrote, "If Negro soldiers are to be drafted into the Army or are to be accepted as volunteers, they must be treated as fellow-soldiers and not as vassals or as racial inferiors."[24] The Office of Facts and Figures reported that of the numerous barriers to full support of the war by Negroes the "fact of discrimination in the armed services of the United States is perhaps the most bitter."

Racial disturbances quieted in 1942 and again increased in intensity in the spring of 1943 in the South, East, and West. Ulysses Lee notes that unlike those of 1941, these disturbances usually involved larger numbers of troops and that Negro troops became aggressors as easily as white troops or civilians. Camp Van Dorn in Mississippi was the site of one of the worst disorders. Some of the men at Camp Van Dorn were involved in earlier disturbances in South Carolina and in Arizona and they were unhappy after being reassigned to Mississippi. Some of them threatened to take over the nearby town. The numerous disturbances resulted in disciplinary actions which delayed the unit's move. Finally, the regiment was transferred for garrison duty in the Aleutians in March 1944.

Camp Stewart, another large post near Savannah, Georgia, also experienced racial disturbances. There, northern Negroes protested the racial segregation of post facilities contrary to War Department orders. They also objected to racial discrimination in the surrounding areas. Negro soldiers clashed with military police when it was falsely reported that a Negro woman had been raped and her husband murdered. A minor incident in a nearby town helped stimulate the clash. Several people were injured and one military policeman was killed. After the riot, a board of investigating officers recommended disbanding an offending battalion and reassigning the men to other organizations. Higher authorities declined and stated that disciplinary procedures were provided for in War Department regulations.

The Army Service Forces continued to study the problem of racial disorders and in January 1944 recommended preventive measures, including the training of more Negro military police, better recreational facilities, equal privileges for Negro officers, measures to eliminate inflammatory and untrue news of racial incidents, and bringing to public attention the lack of established eating and lodging places for Negroes in the South.

---

24 From the *Richmond News Leader,* April 3, 1942.

The disturbances were naturally noted by the highest army authorities, and General Marshall accepted the recommendations of the McCloy Advisory Committee and issued a directive to army commanders. Marshall stressed the influence of rumors in starting disorders, emphasized the importance of following War Department policies with regard to discrimination, and reminded commanders that it was their responsibility to maintain order between soldiers and the civilian population. Marshall ordered commanders to eliminate rumors and propaganda designed to promote unrest.[25] Some army officials recommended censoring and controlling the Negro press. Instead, the public information bureau increased the flow of information concerning the activities of Negro soldiers and thus tried to cultivate better relations with the Negro media. Negro papers used the press releases freely, but in many instances continued their critical reporting. News stories about Negroes in uniform gradually improved the morale of Negro units.

The public information bureau also used other media, and the film *The Negro Soldier,* a carefully prepared and edited production, was widely praised by both whites and Negroes. In 1943, the McCloy Advisory Committee sponsored publication of *Command of Negro Troops,* to increase mutual understanding. Another manual, *Leadership and the Negro Soldier,* was published in October 1944 to achieve the same goal. These documents were intended to increase the fighting strength of the armed forces but they achieved a broader social result.

The army introduced an important policy change; only units were to be segregated, base facilities were opened for the use of all. The directive issued in May 1943 was gradually implemented, there were numerous evasions, but as it was increasingly observed, there was a marked improvement in Negro morale in and out of the army. Toward the end of 1944, officials at Fort Bragg, North Carolina, reported: "No racial discrimination is practiced although there is a general tendency for the units made up of Negro soldiers to use the facilities most convenient to them . . . Negroes may ride on any bus and occupy any seat on the intra-camp of [or] Fort Bragg-Fayetteville service." At Fort Lewis in Washington, it was reported: "Racial relationship continues to be very good at Fort Lewis. No discrimination was observed either on the post or in Tacoma and Seattle."[26]

---

25 General Marshall based his letter to commanders on a more explicit set of recommendations made to him by the McCloy Advisory Committee. Lee, *Employment of Negro Troops,* pp. 381–82.

26 Quotations relating to Fort Bragg and Fort Lewis are in Lee, *Employment of Negro Troops,* p. 400.

Later the Army Service Forces periodically sent teams of investigating officers to check results of the new policy at several installations and made other efforts to improve racial relations. Unfortunately, most Negro soldiers had already completed their training under less desirable circumstances by the time these measures were developed.

The enrollment and training of hundreds of thousands of Negro soldiers and the development of war industries in World Wars I and II each resulted in great internal migrations of Negroes. Soldiers ordinarily had no choice concerning their place of training or future assignment, and in many cases they would not have chosen the places designated. Northern Negroes assigned to southern camps faced an invariably traumatic experience. The southern white in and out of uniform met a new Negro unaccustomed to southern mores and not inclined to adjust to them. The situation forced the army to make modifications in customary white-Negro relationships without trying to change to ways of the South.

The assignment of Negroes to training areas in the North also resulted in new experiences for both races. Life in small agrarian communities was a distinct change for urban northern Negroes, and many northern whites in small towns and communities came in contact with Negroes for the first time. The resulting changes were temporary in most instances, but at least Negroes became better known throughout the United States. In turn, Negroes became more aware of the nation.

Racial segregation was not a feature of the navy during its first century or so, but it became the order of the day during World War I. The navy then began to limit Negroes to service as messmen, aside from letting a few Negroes who served in other branches finish their service. The size of the navy decreased during the postwar period and the number of Negroes in the navy almost reached a vanishing point. The number of Negro messmen also declined and that rating was filled largely by Filipinos. The messman rating was reopened and became the only rating for which Negroes could apply in December 1932, but there were not many volunteers. When the Selective Service and Training Act became law, the secretary of the navy announced that the restrictions on Negroes would continue. Even before American entry into World War II, Negroes attempted to persuade the navy to change its policy.[27] In reply to an inquiry on October 23, 1940, Secretary of

---

27 The best summary of the Negro in the United States Navy in World War II is in Dennis D. Nelson, *The Integration of the Negro into the U.S. Navy* (New York: Farrar, Straus & Young, 1951).

the Navy Knox noted that Negroes could enlist in the messman branch and advance to ratings as cooks and stewards. They would not be regarded as petty officers but would receive the same pay and allowances. Knox wrote:

> Experience of many years in the Navy has shown clearly that men of the colored race, if enlisted in any other branch than the messman branch, and promoted to the position of petty officer, cannot maintain discipline among men of the white race over whom they may be placed by reason of their rating.

Knox concluded that "it would be a waste of time and effort" to train persons in the general service who "by reason of their race and color could not properly and efficiently fill the higher ratings."[28]

Officers of the Negro National Medical Association met with Secretary Knox and Admiral Chester W. Nimitz on January 8, 1941. The admiral said that he was a Texan, but that he "had no prejudice personally," and he bluntly stated that it would be impossible to integrate Negroes into the navy. Nimitz repeated that whites would not tolerate being subordinate to Negroes. One of the Negro doctors suggested a referendum among navy enlisted men, but Admiral Nimitz reportedly said that was "the Soviet way, not the American way." The physician replied that he thought a referendum was the democratic way and Nimitz responded that enlisted men would vote to admit Negroes into the navy but that they would vote overwhelmingly against being subordinate to Negro petty officers.[29]

The navy announced on April 7, 1942, following the United States entry into the war, that Negroes would be accepted in segregated navy, coast guard, and marine units. *Crisis* denigrated the navy's move as a gesture and interpreted the policy to mean that Negroes would be enlisted in labor battalions, limited to shore establishments, and ineligible for commissioned service. The editor was particularly critical of the segregationist aspects of the new policy, but he admitted that the new policy was preferable to the old.[30] The pressure for change continued.

---

28 Frank Knox to Dr. John A. Kenney, October 23, 1940. In National Urban League Files, Series VI, Box 11.

29 Enclosure with letter Eugene Kinckle Jones to Roscoe C. Giles, February 3, 1941. In National Urban League Files, Series VI, Box 11.

30 *Crisis* 49 (May 1942): 151 (editorial). The NAACP was suspicious of the navy's announcement that it would admit Negroes and wrote to Secretary

On February 28, 1943, the war and navy departments announced that Negroes would be inducted into all branches of the armed services and comprise 10 percent of the total complement—in proportion to the number of Negroes in the population. In March it was announced that the quota would apply to the navy and marine corps, and Negro enlistments in the navy then rose from 2,700 to 12,000 per month. The navy soon found it difficult to find places for Negroes in the shore establishments.

The navy then began to assign limited numbers of Negroes to segregated units at sea. On February 23, 1944, the navy announced plans to commission two antisubmarine vessels to be manned by Negro crews. Following the army's example, the navy initially staffed Negro units with white officers and replaced them with Negroes as soon as Negro officers could be trained. These ships were not segregated and the procedure apparently worked to the navy's satisfaction.

There were not enough trained Negro enlisted men and officers to man many vessels completely and the navy began to assign Negroes to twenty-five auxiliary vessels in August 1944. Negroes were not permitted to constitute more than 10 percent of a ship's complement. Again there was no segregation—and no trouble. By October about 500 Negro enlisted men and petty officers were in the navy, mainly in the Pacific Fleet. The navy removed its restrictions on the types of auxiliary craft to which Negroes could be assigned but retained the 10 percent rule in April 1945. The navy dropped separate advanced technical schools for Negroes and whites and trained them together beginning in July 1944 and integrated basic military training a year later. A few months after the war the navy announced:[31]

Knox, informing him of the rumor in Washington that the navy contemplated "recruiting and inducting Negroes as apprentice seamen and later reclassifying and assigning them to duty as messmen." Rear Admiral Randall Jacobs, Chief of Naval Personnel, replied that the navy planned to "enlist Negroes through the Selective Service pursuant to the Executive Order of the President issued December 5, 1942," and he stated that Negroes would be admitted "for general service, in the messman branch, and in construction battalions." Tersely he concluded, "The needs of the Service will dictate the number of men to be channelled into these three branches of the service." Leslie S. Perry, Administrative Assistant, NAACP, to Secretary Knox, March 2, 1943; Randall Jacobs to Perry, March 9, 1942. In NAACP Files, 1943 (270: 5).

31 "Directive 12 December 1945," Secretary of the Navy James Forrestal, cited in Nelson, *Integration of the Negro into the U.S. Navy*, p. 217. See Nelson, pp. 197–226, for a convenient compilation of navy directives and letters, showing the change in the navy's racial policy.

In the administration of naval personnel no *differentiation shall be made because of race or color.* This applies also to authorized personnel in all the armed forces of this country aboard Navy ships or at Navy stations and activities.

The navy ended segregation on February 27, 1946, by ordering that any restrictions "governing types of assignments for which Negro naval personnel are eligible are hereby lifted." The order further stated, "In the utilization of housing, nursing and other facilities, no special or unusual provisions will be made for the accommodation of Negroes."[32]

This brief summary of the evolution toward equal treatment should not obscure the fact that the navy practiced segregation throughout the war. Segregation complicated training in the navy as it did in the army, and the problems which developed in the two services were strikingly similar. Negro sailors were frustrated by segregation and the feeling that they were second class. One historian blamed the commanding officer of the Great Lakes Negro Training Program for using insensitive and archaic methods including "slacker" squads and harsh treatment of recalcitrants. That officer insisted that Negroes sing spirituals on Sunday evenings—a practice that evoked objections from northern Negroes.[33] The commander's techniques, including his insistence that Negro History Week be observed in Negro camps, were an attempt to increase the Negro's pride. The program, however, resulted mainly in irritation.

Many Negroes in the navy were poorly equipped for training. For example, almost 31 percent of those in training at the Great Lakes Training Center in 1944–45 were either illiterate or could not meet the minimum educational standards. The navy's special training unit for illiterates at Camp Peary, Williamsburg, Virginia, found that over 60 percent of the illiterates came from a dozen southern states. The unit provided a minimum education to many Negroes who otherwise would not have had that opportunity. Similarly, Negroes with better educational backgrounds profited from the technical training they received. The school for aviation metalsmiths was one of the most successful.

The Negro in the navy often experienced difficulty despite the training offered. One serious incident occurred on July 17, 1944, at Port Chicago in San Francisco Bay. Two ships loading ammu-

---

32 "Circular Letter 48–46," Chief of Naval Operations, cited in Nelson, *Integration of the Negro into the U.S. Navy,* pp. 219–20.
33 Nelson, *Integration of the Negro into the U.S. Navy,* pp. 28–35.

nition at the docks exploded and more than 300 people were killed and 100 injured. The dead included about 250 Negroes who were working under the guidance of white officers. Most of the injured were Negroes in barracks a mile from the docks.[34]

Survivors were ordered to nearby Vallejo early in August to resume loading ships with ammunition. About 260 Negroes were still unnerved by the Port Chicago explosion and were reluctant to accept another hazardous assignment. Yet all but 44 agreed to go back to work; 6 of these refused to continue after a few days. The navy charged the 50 recalcitrants with mutiny and the ensuing courts-martial found them guilty. They were sentenced to fifteen years hard labor and dishonorable discharge. On review, the commandant of the naval district reduced some of the sentences to eight years on grounds of the men's youth, short service, and otherwise clear records.

Negro leaders and the Negro press strongly objected to the sentences and generally contended that there had been no mutiny. Thurgood Marshall, at that time a leading attorney for the NAACP, asserted:[35]

> The men actually didn't know what happened. Had they been given a direct order to load ammunition, and had then refused to obey that order, then the charges would have been legitimate. But they said no direct order to resume loading was issued them.

Thurgood Marshall subsequently presented a brief personally before the navy's board of review, which finally held that the trial had been fair. The pressure to reverse the court-martial findings continued, and Lester B. Granger, the navy's Negro special aide and adviser to the secretary of the navy, argued for reversal. The navy announced that the convictions had been set aside and the men restored to duty on probation in January 1946. After the Port Chicago incident navy units more carefully selected personnel for ammunition and supply stations formerly "dumping grounds for substandard men," including "illiterates, malcontents, chronic disciplinary cases."[36]

---

34 See Nelson, *Integration of the Negro into the U.S. Navy*, pp. 77–82.

35 As quoted in Nelson, *Integration of the Negro into the U.S. Navy*, p. 79.

36 Nelson, *Integration of the Negro into the U.S. Navy*, pp. 80–81. Another incident occurred in Oxnard, California, where Negro members of a Navy Construction Battalion, or "Seabees," staged a brief hunger strike to protest being passed over for advancement to petty officer ratings. The NAACP took up the cause and forwarded a report to Secretary Forrestal. NAACP Board of Directors Minutes, March 12, 1942, p. 8. In NAACP Files, Series A, Box 12.

Despite the signs of change and responses to pressure, the navy adamantly maintained a racial bias during World War II. The Naval Academy did not have a Negro graduate until 1949. The naval reserve, however, produced significant advances. Young noncommissioned Negro recruiting specialists (chiefs and first-class petty officers) were assigned to recruiting stations in large cities. Many of them were schoolteachers and athletic coaches. The navy also started a training program for Negro officers in January 1944, and sixteen men were selected from the 160,000 Negroes in the navy at that time. The morale of the group was shattered when it was announced that only twelve of the sixteen would be commissioned despite the records, which showed that none was failing at the time.

Many Negroes were subsequently commissioned and most saw active and overseas duty. Generally, Negro naval officers felt they lacked equality of opportunity for advancement, that their assignments were inferior, and that they were the object of discrimination. The commanding officers of the units to which Negro officers were assigned were largely responsible for these conditions. Nevertheless, in the final analysis neither the navy nor the army offered much real opportunity for the development of Negro leaders.

The marine corps, which traditionally had few Negroes, began training the first all-Negro battalion in the summer of 1942 at Camp Lejeune in North Carolina. The always vigilant NAACP publicly protested that the marine corps quota system was unfair to Negroes, especially those on the West Coast. The training class at Camp Lejeune was a success and its graduates were placed in charge of the program—only 10 percent of the class fell into Grade V of the AGCT. The marine corps subsequently increased the proportion of Negro enlistments and began assigning Negroes to its units. The marine corps, however, did not accept, train, or use Negro officers. The first Negro lieutenant in the marine corps was commissioned a few months after World War II.

The coast guard accepted Negroes for service and removed restrictions on officer and enlisted service ratings early in the war. Members of both races were trained together and served together. The first Negro coast guard ensign was commissioned in April 1942. The coast guard was comparatively small and the number of Negroes was correspondingly small. Nevertheless, the coast guard's racial policies were considerably more liberal than those of the other armed services.

CHAPTER 7

Negro in Uniform: Combat

WHEN THE UNITED STATES entered the war, sending Negro troops outside the forty-eight states became a problem. Political and military leaders gave a variety of reasons why Negroes should not be deployed to certain regions.[1] The governors of British West Indian possessions feared the response of their populations to the arrival of well-paid and well-clothed Negro troops. Australia's "White Australia" policy excluded Negroes. The governor of Alaska, Ernest Gruening, believed that mixing Negroes with native Indians and Eskimos would be bad. The air corps opposed sending Negroes to Iceland, Greenland, and Labrador. The Mormon Church objected to Negro troops in Mormon communities.[2] Liberia did not want American Negroes because they would enjoy preferred status in comparison to the Liberian population. These protests were referred to Secretary of War Stimson, and he created a simple guiding rule: Negroes would not be sent to countries where they were not wanted if the United States had asked to send troops to that country. Otherwise, the army would determine where Negroes would go. Initially, Stimson went along with

---

[1] Ulysses Lee, *The Employment of Negro Troops*, The United States Army in World War II: Special Studies (Washington, D.C.: U.S. Government Printing Office, 1966), pp. 429–31.

[2] Joseph Anderson, Secretary to the First Presidency, Church of Jesus Christ of Latter-Day Saints, Salt Lake City, explained the church's views in a letter to Ira De A. Reid, Consultant on Minorities, War Manpower Commission. He stated that Negroes who already lived in the intermountain region had been and would continue to be unmolested. He continued, "I am directed, however, to say to you that the Church would view with great anxiety the presence of Negroes in any considerable numbers in its communities because it would bring into them an element which does not, as a group, conform to the standards of life of the church. . . ." Anderson wrote that the church stood "absolutely" against sexual intermingling of the white and the colored race, "whether such intermingling is the result of legitimate marriage or illicit relationship." Consequently, the church would "look with great apprehension upon the presence of Negroes in its communities and would discourage such presence in all lawful ways." Anderson to Reid, March 9, 1943. In NAACP Files, 1943 (270:5). It appears that neither Reid nor Walter White decided to pursue the matter further at the time. Anderson's letter was in response to a query by Reid. See also Reid to White, March 18, 1943, in this same file.

the stereotyped idea that Negroes should not be sent to far northern places, but they were later used to aid in the construction of
the Alcan Highway.

The movement of Negro troops overseas was slowed despite the
Stimson rule. For example, only Negro service units were initially
sent to the United Kingdom. Australian officials requested that
Negroes already sent to Australia be returned to the United States
or deployed elsewhere. General Marshall asked General Mac-
Arthur for his views, and MacArthur replied that by using the
troops "in the front zones away from great centers of population"
he could "minimize the difficulties involved and yet use to advantage those already dispatched."[3]

By the end of 1942, Negro troops sent abroad were proportionately fewer than their numbers in the overall strength of the army.
The inspector general, Major General Virgil L. Peterson, and his
assistant, General Davis, questioned whether it was advisable to
continue training and equipping Negro units that could not be
used in the different theaters. The Selective Service System, however, continued to pour men into the army and the question was
rejected. The arguments over the deployment of Negro troops
continued in staff studies and surveys. It was argued that Negro
soldiers should not be sent to Caribbean bases because their standard of living was higher than that of the local population, but
the counterargument noted that the standard of living of white
troops was also higher. It was also argued that Negroes were better
adapted to the tropics and that white soldiers could be released for
duty elsewhere. The domestic friction between Negro and white
soldiers in 1941 and 1942 led a few observers to contend that
Negro troops should not be sent to any foreign country.

The army gave specialized training to troops assigned to areas
with great extremes of weather, but many Negroes sent to work
on the Alcan Highway were unaccustomed to subzero weather and
found it difficult to adjust to the cold climate and isolation. The
higher pay given to civilians increased the Negro's discontent with
working on the road.[4] A contingent of Negroes sent to the Belgian Congo adjusted to the weather readily but had distasteful
racial restrictions imposed on them by Belgian authorities. The
troop buildup in Great Britain for the invasion of Europe resulted

---

[3] As quoted in Lee, *Employment of Negro Troops*, p. 432.

[4] See Stetson Conn, Rose C. Engelman, and Byron Fairchild, *Guarding the
United States and Its Outposts*, The United States Army in World War II:
The Western Hemisphere (Washington, D.C.: U.S. Government Printing
Office, 1964), p. 408.

in considerable friction between Negro and white troops. The British had never relished the immigration of Negroes from their own possessions, yet many British citizens resented the attitude of white American soldiers toward the Negro. The British objected to the imposition of white American mores on their society.

Criticism by Negroes centered on their slow rate of deployment and Jim Crow practices in overseas theaters. The National Urban League's *Opportunity* noted that a booklet distributed to American soldiers stationed in England was "another don't book." "Its contents," wrote the editor, "consist largely of admonitions in the form of don'ts, with simple explanations of the differences in the customs and character of the English and American people." The pamphlet first advised soldiers, "when you see a man in the uniform of the United States Army, no matter what his color or race, he is your comrade in arms, facing the same dangers you face, fighting for the same things you are fighting for," and then proceeded to list the don'ts:

> Don't degrade him by the use of degrading epithets such as "nigger."
> Don't attempt to exclude him from any place open to other American soldiers.
> Don't attempt to philosophize on the race question. The Army doesn't need philosophers but fighters and you may get mixed up.
> Don't defend lynching when some of our Allies question you about this uncivilized practice. It is indefensible.

The editor of *Opportunity* commented, "We think such a book with a few modifications for home consumption, is imperative."[5]

Relatively few Negro combat troops were sent to the front in 1942. The 24th Infantry Regiment was sent to the New Hebrides in anticipation of an advance to Guadalcanal, but it arrived after the heavy fighting was over. There was talk of deploying a Negro regiment to Hawaii as its main defense but there were several objections raised. General Davis felt that Negroes were concerned over the army's failure to give Negro soldiers a chance to fight. He formally recommended to the McCloy Advisory Committee in April 1943 that it propose sending a Negro combat unit immediately to a forward area.[6]

---

5 *Opportunity* 20 (August 1942): 226. Walter White exerted pressure for such pamphlets. White to Secretary of War Stimson, October 9, 1942; Lt. Col. Page to White, October 23, 1942. White had also conferred with Page and Hastie. In NAACP Files, 1942 (264:2).

6 Lee, *Employment of Negro Troops,* p. 450.

The air corps' 99th Pursuit Squadron, sent to North Africa in April 1943, was the first Negro unit to see combat, and it became involved in controversy. Lieutenant General Carl Spaatz, commander of the Fifth Air Force in North Africa, refused to rush the unit into action despite the attention given it by the press. The squadron later participated in attacks on Pantelleria, and Lieutenant Colonel Benjamin O. Davis, Jr., squadron commander, was relieved of command in August and returned to the United States to command and train a new fighter group.

General Spaatz received official reports on the squadron which suggested that it was inferior to white units in combat. The group commander, for example, reported that formation flying was "very satisfactory until jumped by enemy aircraft, when the squadron seems to disintegrate." He also noted that Colonel Davis asked that his men be taken out of combat for three days because of fatigue during the campaign in Sicily and that white pilots in combat longer had kept flying. General Spaatz forwarded the reports to General H. H. Arnold, chief of army air forces, with a moderating statement that he had personally visited the squadron and that there had "been no question of their ground discipline and their general conduct." Spaatz concluded, however, that the analysis of the squadron had been fair: "I feel that no squadron has been introduced into this theatre with a better background of training than had by the 99th Fighter Squadron."[7]

The report was particularly damaging because it seemingly indicated that Negro units were inferior even when they had been well trained. Consequently, it was recommended that Negro fighter squadrons be assigned to rear defense areas and that the training of Negroes for a proposed medium bomber group be dropped. The long period of training given Negro pursuit pilots was thus cited against them.

General Marshall received the recommendations in October 1943 and ordered a complete review of Negro units in combat; questionnaires were sent to commandants in all areas. Commanders in the South Pacific reported that Negro units were kept in rear areas subject only to occasional bombings. The report indicated that Negro officers and men were not as effective as whites. Commands in the Southwest Pacific reported that no Negro units were in combat but that service troops had performed well under fire—Negro officers were rated as average.

---

7 Quotations in this paragraph are from Lee, *Employment of Negro Troops*, pp. 453–55.

One Negro unit in India, the 823d Engineer Aviation Battalion, had been under fire and its conduct was reported as magnificent. Reports on Negro service units in North Africa ranged from satisfactory to less than satisfactory. General Eisenhower praised the maligned 99th Fighter Squadron for its strafing attacks in Sicily and noted that engineer and antiaircraft ground units had performed well. Significantly, Eisenhower's report suggested that Negro units had not been tested enough in battle to support any conclusions regarding their performance.

Colonel Davis informed the advisory committee that the 99th Pursuit Squadron had made early errors and had experienced lack of confidence, but he was convinced that the situation improved later. The investigation continued and it was reported that, if there had not been enough testing of Negroes in combat on the ground, there had been in the air. The report recommended that Negro air units not be used in active areas.[8]

The air corps then faced the problem of what to do with the Negro medium bomber unit in training for combat duty. General Arnold decided on October 27, 1943, that the group would continue training and be deployed to North Africa. Meanwhile, the 99th Fighter Squadron remained on duty in Italy. There was little combat there during this stage of the war, but the squadron was heavily engaged in flight operations. The squadron built self-confidence and eventually gained recognition within the 79th Fighter Group. Additional Negro fighter units were sent to Italy in 1944.

The use of Negro ground units in combat presented continuing problems. Negro groups insisted that Negro troops be given a fair share of action, yet commanders were reluctant to accept Negro troops. Lieutenant General Millard F. Harmon, commanding army forces in the South Pacific, argued in 1943 that his logistic problems—long distances and transportation difficulties—demanded only the most effective troops. Harmon's need for manpower was so great, however, that he agreed to use one Negro regiment in combat and to garrison forward areas if white troops were unavailable.[9]

The backlog of Negro units in the United States had increasingly adverse effects on morale—particularly when the army began converting combat infantry for service in engineer and artillery units. Negro leaders questioned the War Department about the

---

8 Lee, *Employment of Negro Troops,* pp. 456–61.
9 Lee, *Employment of Negro Troops,* p. 471.

conversion and Secretary Stimson's reply increased Negro discontent. Stimson asserted that the selection of units to be changed "had been based solely on the relative abilities, capabilities and status of training for the personnel in the units available for conversion." He added, "It so happens that a relatively large percentage of the Negroes inducted in the Army have fallen within the lower educational classifications, and many of the Negro units accordingly have been unable to master efficiently the techniques of modern weapons."[10]

Truman K. Gibson, Jr., Hastie's successor as civilian aide to Secretary Stimson, predicted that Stimson's letter would produce an outraged response. Gibson also objected because the letter was not referred to him or the advisory committee for comment before it was distributed. Gibson's prophecy was correct; the Negro press reacted bitterly, and an editorial in *Crisis* termed Stimson's letter "probably the most inept letter of the war" and one "which has infuriated Negro Americans as has no other single incident since Pearl Harbor."[11]

The Stimson statement and the resulting protests focused attention on the problem of what to do about Negro combat troops. The McCloy Advisory Committee studied the problem in February 1944 and recommended in early March "that, as soon as possible, colored Infantry, Field Artillery, and other Combat units be introduced into combat . . . and that schedules if necessary be changed."[12] The commitment of Negro units to battle thus resulted from public and political pressure rather than the requests of commanders in the field. Commanders accepted the recommendations only when it was clear that Negroes would be sent to forward areas.

The preparation and deployment of troops for combat were complicated and at times confusing. In general, the quality of preparation and training determined how troops would perform in the field. Poor training resulted in unsatisfactory performance, and large, well-trained units usually performed well. The attendant publicity and the views of critics and supporters made the task of unit commanders even more difficult. Consequently, according to Ulysses Lee, the career of Negro troops was atypical.

Negro units went into action in the Pacific and reacted as did

---

10 Stimson to Representative Hamilton Fish, quoted in Lee, *Employment of Negro Troops,* pp. 475–76.

11 *Crisis* 51 (April 1944): 104.

12 Cited in Lee, *Employment of Negro Troops,* p. 482.

other newly trained units. Assistant Secretary McCloy summarized one report: "Although they show some important limitations, on the whole I feel that the report is not so bad as to discourage us." He continued by citing the performance of the 99th Fighter Squadron: "You remember that they were not very good, but that Squadron has now taken its place in the line and has performed very well."[13] Stimson agreed but in his opinion Negro troops would succeed only with white officers.

The 99th Fighter Squadron gradually changed its image in the European theater. The squadron performed well in the air fighting over Anzio, and Major General John K. Cannon, earlier quite critical, told the men of the 79th Fighter Group and the 99th Fighter Squadron, "It's a grand show. You're doing a magnificent job."[14] The actions of the Negro pilots were broadly covered and strongly praised in the press.[15] *Crisis* reported that the fliers were "no longer on trial . . . they have now assumed a position of leadership in combat and pursuit."[16]

The 93d Division advanced from island to island in the Pacific, usually engaged in rearguard and sometimes "mopping up" actions. Ulysses Lee summarized its work: "Whether or not the Division moved to the asset side depended largely on the viewer and his interpretation of the value of doing unglamorous but necessary work."[17]

The Negro 370th Regimental Combat Team weeded out substandard men and replaced them with volunteers during training. Its morale was high and it was deployed to Italy, where it was warmly welcomed. The team moved into action, and at first had the advantage of following a retreating enemy that offered little resistance. Observers noted that the soldiers acted as any new unit might in the limited action—they were not aggressive but seemed responsive to learning the art of war. The real test came in an attack on a vigorously held German position (the Gothic Line) in heavy rain and mud. After a month of fierce combat, the team's morale deteriorated. A few instances of individual heroism were reported, but officers noted that the troops had a tendency to panic and in some cases they refused to continue the attack.

13 As quoted in Lee, *Employment of Negro Troops*, pp. 516–17.
14 As quoted in Lee, *Employment of Negro Troops*, p. 517.
15 For a summary of press accounts, see *Monthly Summary of Events and Trends in Race Relations* 1:3 (October 1943): 21–22.
16 *Crisis* 51 (March 1944): 83.
17 Lee, *Employment of Negro Troops*, p. 529.

Many of the officers were killed or wounded and leadership became a real problem. The commander of the 370th wrote, "Morale went down, esprit de corps departed, determined resistance on the part of the enemy began, difficult terrain was encountered, and so the natural result was that combat efficiency was lowered."[18]

The arrival of the rest of the 92d Division did not help the situation because there was serious disaffection between its soldiers and their officers. An investigating officer recommended that the commanding officer be removed, but the recommendation was rejected. Since both sides were on the defensive, nothing of consequence occurred for a brief period. It was thus decided to reorganize and shift some of the units from the front lines. While these changes were being made, Gibson paid a visit to the Italian front at the invitation of General Mark Clark. Gibson talked with hundreds of officers and enlisted men in an attempt to find the facts and the reasons for the team's failures.

Gibson held a press conference in Rome on March 14, 1945, arranged by the army's public relations officer at the request of war correspondents. In this conference Gibson reported what he had already told army officials. He acknowledged that "there have been many withdrawals by panic stricken Infantrymen," and stated that there were also "many acts of individual and group bravery." He noted that there was an "unsatisfactory promotion policy" for Negro officers, and that the command maintained a racist attitude. In addition, Gibson noted that there was a large percentage of Negro soldiers in Grades IV and V who had come from civilian backgrounds where there was little chance for the "inculcation of pride in self or even love of country."[19]

Newspapers like the *New York Times* praised Gibson for his candor, but the Negro press reacted strongly against his reports. *Crisis* published a lengthy editorial entitled "Negro Soldier Betrayed" and excoriated Gibson. The editor asked,

> If the 92d Division is made of 92% illiterates and near-illiterates, whose fault is it? Certainly not the Negroes. . . . Why would the War Department, if it really wanted to give a fair test, send a division into the front lines with 92 out of every 100 men in the two lowest classifications? The 92d was licked before it started.

The editor continued,

---

18 Cited in Lee, *Employment of Negro Troops*, p. 552.
19 As quoted in Lee, *Employment of Negro Troops*, pp. 576–77.

It must be remembered that these men were beaten up by bus drivers, shot up by military and civilian police, insulted by their white officers, denied transportation to and from the post, restricted to certain post exchanges, and jim crowed in post theatres.

The editor concluded that segregation was the root cause and recommended that the War Department move as quickly as possible "to wipe out segregation of fighting men according to color."[20]

The 92d Division went into the spring offensive of 1945 greatly changed in character. It included a white regiment, an American-Japanese regiment, and a virtually new Negro regiment with officers of both races. The fighting went well at the outset, but some of the original officers were killed and the situation deteriorated. A few individual units and men distinguished themselves for ability and heroism, but elsewhere in the division morale was low. Some Negroes believed the introduction of white troops implied that Negroes could not fight by themselves. Negroes in other units expressed the hope that they would not be judged by the poor showing of the 92d Division.[21]

Only about 2 percent of all the Negroes in the army were in the 92d Division. Most Negroes were in the service forces, which operated in small units attached to large white groups. Negroes thus performed a variety of duties throughout the world. They were involved in the major campaigns in Europe and the Pacific and in a host of other places from Alaska to Liberia. Negroes served in the quartermaster corps, as engineers, in antiaircraft batteries, and in port and amphibious truck companies. They operated smoke generators at the front and served in ambulance companies. "The sheer quantity of work performed by Negro troops," wrote Ulysses Lee, "often operating on round-the-clock schedules, was tremendous."[22] Their performance was not perfect, but in general they maintained a good record in service and in their relations with white troops and with the people of foreign countries.

From the standpoint of Negroes and whites alike, one of the most satisfactory records was achieved by Negroes in the artillery and armored units which served in Europe. They were outstand-

---

20 *Crisis* 52 (April 1945): 97 (editorial). The Board of Directors of the NAACP voted to censure Gibson. NAACP Board of Directors Minutes, May 14, 1945, p. 6. In NAACP Files, Series A, Box 12.

21 Lee, *Employment of Negro Troops,* p. 589.

22 Lee, *Employment of Negro Troops,* p. 592.

ing in the Ardennes campaign during the German counteroffensive. After the siege of Bastogne, Major General Maxwell D. Taylor, commanding the 101st Airborne, wrote to the commander of the Negro 969th Battalion expressing appreciation for its "gallant support." He stated, "This Division is proud to have shared the Battlefield with your command."[23] Tank battalions and tank destroyer crews also distinguished themselves in the European campaign. One tank destroyer battalion performed badly and a subsequent investigation showed that it was manned with an excessive number of soldiers from low AGCT grades.

A very significant breakthrough almost occurred toward the end of 1944. High army officials decided to accept Negro volunteers as individual infantry replacements due to a critical shortage of infantry riflemen replacements. Late in December the army called for volunteers:[24]

> To this end the Commanding General, Com Z, is happy to offer to a limited number of colored troops who have had infantry training, the privilege of joining our veteran units at the front to deliver the knockout blow . . . your comrades at the front are anxious to share the glory of victory with you. Your relatives and friends everywhere have been urging that you be granted this privilege.

The notice ended by expressing confidence in Negro volunteers.

When news of the plan reached Supreme Headquarters, Allied Expeditionary Force (SHAEF), Lieutenant Walter Bedell Smith saw that calling for introduction of volunteers into units "without regard to color" might embarrass the War Department, and he protested to General Eisenhower. Eisenhower rewrote the directive deleting that reference to color, leaving the inference that Negroes would be assigned to Negro units and that if the supply was greater than the need "these men will be suitably incorporated in other organizations so that their service and their fighting spirit may be efficiently utilized.[25]

More than 4,560 Negro troops volunteered in response to the original notice before it was replaced by Eisenhower's revision—the original plan was to accept 2,000.[26] It is difficult to estimate

---

23 Cited in Lee, *Employment of Negro Troops*, p. 651.

24 Cited in Lee, *Employment of Negro Troops*, p. 689.

25 This draft, dated January 4, 1945, appears in Dwight D. Eisenhower, *The Papers of Dwight David Eisenhower: The War Years*, vol. 4 (Baltimore: Johns Hopkins Press, 1970), p. 2394.

26 Roland G. Ruppenthal, *Logistical Support of the Armies*, The United States Army in World War II: The European Theater of Operations (Wash-

what the response would have been if the volunteers had known that they would be placed in small segregated units rather than integrated individually into white units. The men went through retraining and were assigned in platoons to fight with white troops. Their motivation was high, and the men were welcomed as needed allies at the front; there was less enthusiasm in quiet sectors. General Davis later traveled through the Twelfth Army Area and received good reports on the volunteers. Volunteers not quite as well trained also did well with the 6th Army Group and the Seventh Army. Ulysses Lee summarized: "In the Negro Infantry rifle platoons, the employment of Negro troops moved farthest from traditional Army patterns."[27]

The secretary of the NAACP, Walter White, was one of the most effective "watchdogs" of the army's treatment of Negroes in uniform. He frequently criticized the problems encountered by Negro soldiers in the United States. In 1942, for example, he corresponded with the War Department and charged that white officers slandered Negroes in uniform. Stimson responded by writing, "While I share your concern over these problems, I am unable to think of them as ones which can readily be alleviated by the issuance of military orders, or other direct action from the War Department."[28] White heard rumors of continuing racial difficulties in England and the European theater and decided to see for himself. Assistant Secretary of War John J. McCloy and other high officials in the War Department favored White's trip, and the *New York Post* provided the means by asking that White be accredited as a war correspondent.[29] White then flew to England via Newfoundland in an army transport command plane. He interviewed army personnel in England, from privates to General Eisenhower, and visited North Africa and Italy. On his return, White wrote *A Rising Wind* about his experiences. The press widely circulated his report to the War Department, which listed fourteen recommendations.[30] White's recommendations centered

---

ington, D.C.: Office of the Chief of Military History, Department of the Army, 1959), pp. 322–23; Lee, *Employment of Negro Troops,* p. 693.

[27] Lee, *Employment of Negro Troops,* p. 703.

[28] Stimson to White, September 3, 1942. See also Stimson to White, May 22, 1942; White to Stimson, August 18, 1942. In NAACP Files, 1942 (264:2). On another occasion White objected to the addition of segregated hospitals. White to W. Harry Haller, October 11, 1944. In NAACP Files, 1945 (359:5).

[29] Walter White, *A Rising Wind* (New York: Doubleday, Doran, 1945), p. 12.

[30] A detailed listing of White's recommendations is in NAACP Board of Directors Minutes, May 8, 1944. In NAACP Files, Series A, Box 12. The NAACP paid the expenses for the trip. NAACP Board of Directors Minutes, September 13, 1943. In NAACP Files, Series A, Box 11.

on the social treatment of Negro soldiers; and he proposed that the army eliminate off limit signs for Negro soldiers, cut down on anti-Negro rumors being spread among the civilian population (these were greatest in England and in Italy), and do away with racist paternalism on the part of white officers. White suggested that orientation lectures would be of help to white officers and men going abroad.

White also dealt with the army's treatment of Negroes and urged the appointment of a special board of review for court-martial cases to determine the validity of the belief of many Negroes that Negroes were "punished more quickly and more severely than white soldiers." White recommended that the board include an eminent Negro lawyer of appropriate rank. White strongly recommended that more Negro combat troops be sent to England to offset the rumors being circulated that Negroes were afraid to fight. In addition, he proposed that Negro and white fighter squadrons function in the same groups. He forcefully commented on the military police, noted that white military police bore arms and Negro military police did not, and recommended that only military police guarding payrolls be armed. White requested more news about Negro troops and more sympathetic treatment by military censors to give Negro civilians at home a better picture of what their men were doing. Finally, White told the War Department that it was lagging behind "much of the personnel of the Army," and advised that while a more progressive position would meet opposition, it would be approved by "a much larger percentage" than the War Department might think possible.

White's trip, supported by high-level officials, and his strong recommendations are significant for several reasons. First, the War Department's interest in improving the lot of the Negro soldier arose primarily from military considerations and not from social or humanitarian concerns. The department wanted to create the most effective fighting force possible. Second, the secretary of a largely Negro pressure group had obviously made significant progress by traveling to the theaters of war with the army's cooperation, talking with generals, and coming home to tell the War Department what to do. Third, White's views were essentially moderate, he believed his reforms would improve the status of the Negro in the army and also make the army a more effective fighting machine. Finally, White attempted, consciously or unconsciously, to build Negro morale. He proudly noted, for example, that the British liked American Negroes better than American whites after getting acquainted and disabusing themselves of false rumors. He also proudly noted that Negro men were especially popular with European women.

White later traveled to the Pacific area and performed a comparable task for Negro servicemen there.[31] He arrived on Guam following a period of friction between Negro naval personnel and white marines which resulted in some fatalities. Some Negro base company personnel were arrested, and White appeared as their counsel in the subsequent hearings, which lasted three weeks. He left Guam before the board of inquiry had made its report, and on returning to Washington, he asked Secretary James Forrestal for a copy. Forrestal declined on the ground that disclosure or discussion would not be appropriate, since he would be required to act on the record. White refused to let the matter rest and obtained an interview with President Truman to discuss the Guam incident and other issues. At Truman's request White sent the president a memorandum on the affair.[32]

---

[31] Walter White, *A Man Called White: The Autobiography of Walter White* (New York: Viking Press, 1948), pp. 277–93.

[32] White to President Truman, May 26, 1945. In NAACP Files, 1945 (359:2). In this same box is a summary of the meeting between President Truman and White. The president expressed an interest in a further meeting, and White suggested that other Negro leaders also be invited.

CHAPTER 8

Negro Women

TWO MAJOR FACTORS, urbanization and war, affected the status of American Negro women during the first half of the twentieth century. Generally, the lot of Negro women in the agrarian South was hard; most of them lived in the country and labored in field and home in a ceaseless struggle against poverty. They also worked at very low wages as household servants in towns and cities. A relatively few middle-class and upper-class Negro women did not have to contribute to family support, although some worked to increase family income. Negro women had to accommodate themselves to the customs of white society. They typically accepted racist restrictions or retired into small circles of friends to avoid contact with whites.

World War I began a mass movement of Negroes to the North and to urban areas. The men were the first to leave in large numbers, and the responsibilities of the women left behind, already the financial mainstays of many families, became even greater. When the men found reasonably steady employment their families joined them, and some of the families which had subsisted on the mother's income now came to rely on the father as the main breadwinner. Urbanization frequently broke up families— husbands deserted their families and defaulted on family responsibilities in growing numbers. Overcrowded housing was almost as great a problem. Nearly a third of Negro families took in lodgers to increase their incomes, and family life was thus disrupted. There was a lack of privacy, and the limited space in the typical Negro home forced children into the streets in search of something to do.[1]

Urbanization especially affected the young, single Negro woman. Her role was well established in the southern agrarian family, where a flexible, augmented family system left room for unmarried daughters, aunts, and nieces. Single women had no difficulty finding work in the fields or as domestic servants. In northern cities the family unit was not so accommodating, espe-

---

[1] A principal source on the Negro family is E. Franklin Frazier, *The Negro Family in the United States* (Chicago: University of Chicago Press, 1939), See also Andrew Billingsley, *Black Families in White America* (Englewood Cliffs, N.J.: Prentice-Hall, 1968).

cially during the period of adjustment to urban life. Apartments were crowded and extra rooms were usually occupied by paying lodgers rather than nonpaying female relatives. Attitudes toward illegitimacy were different in the North. Children born out of wedlock in the agrarian South were easily accepted as part of the augmented family and no particular stigma was attached to the children or their mothers; children merely added to the family's capacity for work. In large cities, however, illegitimate children were unwanted, and unwed mothers and their children were made to feel ashamed. Therefore, for Negro women in the North, avoiding pregnancy out of wedlock became very important. During the interwar period, jobs were hard to find, and poorly educated Negro women had few opportunities.

Statistics indicate that during the first half of 1935 in Harlem 6,540 Negro men and 1,338 Negro women were arrested. Over two-thirds of the women were between the ages of 21 and 30, and almost 80 percent were arrested for immoral sexual behavior. E. Franklin Frazier commented, "In an environment like Harlem, where there was little opportunity for employment for a large number of single women who had broken away from the family immoral conduct offered a means of livelihood."[2] It should be noted that a majority of Negro women in Harlem were welcome members of their families despite the economic hardships. They attended school and, in due course, took advantage of federal programs instituted by the National Youth Administration to obtain vocational training.

Apart from lower classes trapped in urban slums, the experience of middle-class and upper-class Negro women paralleled that of white women of comparable status. In September 1942, *Crisis* published a series of full-page photographs of the "First Ladies of Colored America" in tribute to the influence of Negro women. The introduction stated: "Indeed, the colored woman has been a more potent factor in shaping Negro society than the white woman has been in shaping white society because the sexual caste system has been much more fluid and ill defined than among whites." The article cited the criteria used to select "first ladies" and continued, "Through the church, fraternal organizations, parent-teachers associations, NAACP branches and various social groups, our women have welded a weak and divided people into a more compact, harmonious and increasingly powerful group."[3]

2 E. Franklin Frazier, *The Negro in the United States*, rev. ed. (New York: Macmillan, 1957), pp. 630–37.

3 *Crisis* 49 (September 1942): 287.

The series ran for fourteen months with four photographs in each issue. The women selected generally had attended either an eastern college or a southern Negro institution and taught school for a number of years. They married physicians or heads of Negro schools and colleges and were active in various social organizations, churches, schools, and political groups. Some of the selectees were successful theatrical or concert artists and many were involved in social welfare programs. One started and directed a school for delinquent girls, and another headed a private school for Negro children. Some had successful business careers, often in partnership with their husbands. The business enterprises included a candymaking company in Alabama, an undertaking business in Louisiana, a publishing company in Pennsylvania, a fox farm in Alaska, and a chain of beauty colleges throughout the country. Some of the selectees held public office, a first for Negro women; one was a deputy collector of internal revenue in New York and another a member of the Pennsylvania House of Representatives. Practically all of them were public-spirited citizens who devoted time and effort to charitable enterprises.

Few of the women were known outside their own regions or by whites. There were exceptions; Mary McLeod Bethune was the leading female representative of her race at that time. Her reputation as an educator and as head of Bethune-Cookman College and her work in Washington before and during World War II made Bethune a national figure.[4] Marian Anderson, to whom Arturo Toscanini once said, "A voice like yours is heard only once in a thousand years," was also widely known.[5] Hattie McDaniel, well known for her various roles in films, especially *Gone With the Wind,* was a popular artist. Two stage stars made the list, Anne Brown and Etta Moten, both of whom had played Bess in the musical, *Porgy and Bess.*

Issues of *Crisis* honoring the "first ladies" also featured several women. However, the covers featured women who were uniformly young and attractive, and the covers also made it clear that there was a war going on. Etta Moten was the only "first lady" to be featured on a cover. The only other well-known performer to appear on a cover was singer Lena Horne. The others were not well known as individuals but rather represented easily recognizable types: the army nurse, the WAC, the canteen hostess, the war worker, the College Co-ed Farmer for Victory. In other words,

---

4 For an extended account of Mrs. Bethune's work, see Rackham Holt, *Mary McLeod Bethune: A Biography* (Garden City, N.Y.: Doubleday, 1964).

5 As quoted in *Crisis* 49 (October 1942): 303.

Crisis presented Negro women in roles similar to those of other American women who were aiding the war effort in a variety of ways.

Crisis cover features symbolized the efforts of Negro women engaged in all kinds of war work. An article in *Opportunity* noted: "It took a war to wedge open job opportunities for Negroes that heretofore have been advertised 'For Whites Only.' More and more women by the thousands are being placed in jobs formerly held by men."[6] The writer then described the training programs offered by the Harlem YWCA Trade School in New York City. Women in this school were trained as stenographers, bookkeepers, power machine operators, switchboard operators, and file clerks. The school also acted as a guidance and placement agency.

Government agencies like the National Youth Administration offered similar training programs throughout the country to meet mounting demands for labor, and Negro women shared in the expansion. Another article in *Opportunity* noted three trends in the employment of Negro women.[7] First, more Negro women were entering war production and other types of jobs as well; they were serving as waitresses, elevator operators, and power-sewing-machine operators. Second, a much higher percentage of Negro women were completing high school and college educations than was the case in 1918. Third, many women joined labor unions, as dues-paying members and active participants.

The National Urban League noted the trends in women's work in *Opportunity* and encouraged Negro women and men to enter war work. The journal also advised women on their working conduct and dress. The prospective woman war worker was advised that "the neat, clean, sensibly dressed woman rates ten to one in war job placements over the glamour girl." Women were advised that war work did not necessarily mean "dead end jobs," and it was predicted that the factories which produced war materials would manufacture "radios, refrigerators, and washing machines" in time of peace.[8]

The obstacles which initially confronted Negro women seeking

---

6 Mattie Julian-Brown, "Train Today for Today's Jobs!" *Opportunity* 20 (May 1942): 138.

7 Mary Anderson, "Negro Women on the Production Front," *Opportunity* 21 (April 1943): 38.

8 LeRoy W. Jeffries, "Step Up, Lady—Want a War Job?" *Opportunity* 21 (April 1943): 40, 41, 91.

war jobs were similar to those that had blocked Negro men. Company policies opposed hiring Negroes; separate toilet facilities had not been built; applicants were overqualified for jobs; factories maintained "proper" proportions of Negroes to whites; and Negro quotas were already filled. The FEPC, labor, and management eventually removed some of these barriers, mainly due to increasing needs for skilled and unskilled labor. The United States Employment Service handled about 14 percent of the hirings in industry, and its stance helped establish the procedures for others. *Opportunity* quickly noted those agencies that refused to hire Negroes and thus pressured for change. It was pointed out, for example, that the public utilities in Pittsburgh, a city with 115,-000 Negroes, failed to hire Negro women to fill many types of jobs. The journal also charged that Western Electric, H. J. Heinz, and other companies were hiring very few Negro women.[9]

The Women's Bureau in the Department of Labor was concerned with Negro women in industry, and it published several guides for women at work in factories and on farms. The bureau was also interested in removing inequities and it supported organized labor's demands for equal pay for equal labor. Women, however, found that there were loopholes in government regulations and usually blamed management for the resulting inequities. One such loophole resulted from the practice of calling a job by another name (e.g., "out of title" work). Thus a secretary or an assistant would perform the work of an executive at a much lower wage. Such wage differences were rationalized on the grounds that men would object to women receiving the same pay because women "did not take their work as seriously as men" or because the cost of special facilities should be offset by paying lower wages to women. The Women's Bureau challenged these arguments, but it should be noted that statistics verified that the rate of absenteeism was higher for women than for men. The home responsibilities of women and their need to take time for shopping were cited as causes, and efforts were made to reduce absenteeism.

Men were drafted into military service in increasing numbers, and as production demands increased, job opportunities for women rose. Many factories hired unskilled workers and instituted on-the-job training. Some companies actually preferred

---

[9] George E. DeMar, "Negro Women Are American Workers, Too," *Opportunity* 21 (April 1943): 43, 77.

ing "green" employees rather than retraining semiskilled
,onnel,[10] and the entrance of women into the work force pro-
:ed other problems. Many women were married, they had to
ep their families going, find babysitters or locate nurseries and
ıy care centers. It was estimated that over 2 million Negro
women were working in January 1945 and that 70 percent of
them were still in service occupations. Their employment, however, shifted from household service and more of them became
beauticians, waitresses, and cooks. There were 50,000 more Negro women in domestic service in 1944 than in 1940, and there
was a marked increase in government employment during the
same period.[11]

Negro women benefited from the greatly increased demand for
nurses brought on by the war despite certain obstacles. For example, there was a shortage of training facilities. Negro colleges attended to this problem, and by 1945 five institutions had schools
or departments of nursing, while numerous others offered pre-
nursing instruction. The National Nursing Council for War
Service, representing a large number of nursing and teaching organizations, tried to expedite the entrance of Negro women into
various types of nursing needed in the war effort. Radio programs
stimulated enrollment, and the federal government provided
funds to extend financial aid to prospective nurses, commencing
in 1941. The council also arranged institutes in New York and
Chicago for directors of schools to study problems connected with
the education and distribution of Negro students.[12]

The war effort gradually opened hospital doors which formerly
had been closed to Negroes—notably the Philadelphia General
Hospital and the Kings County and Cumberland hospitals in
Brooklyn, New York. The commissioner of hospitals in New
York announced in 1943 that no nursing school operated by New
York City could refuse to admit Negroes on the basis of race.[13]

The need for nurses in the armed services naturally increased
as the war progressed. Negro nurses played a small role in World
War I; only 18 Negro army nurses were called to duty. World
War II found about 200 trained Negro nurses in army uniform

---

[10] Charles C. Berkley, "War Work—A Challenge to Negro Womanpower,"
Opportunity 21 (April 1943): 59.

[11] Cited in *Monthly Summary of Events and Trends in Race Relations* 2:7
(February 1945): 186. See also Robert C. Weaver, *Negro Labor: A National
Problem* (New York: Harcourt, Brace, 1946), pp. 81–82.

[12] Estelle Massey Riddle, "The Negro Nurse and the War," *Opportunity*
21 (April 1943): 44–45, 92.

[13] Riddle, "The Negro Nurse," pp. 45, 93.

by January 1943, mostly as second lieutenants. More than half were assigned to Fort Huachuca in Arizona, but they came from all over the country, from private nursing, public health work, and service in hospitals.[14]

Negro physicians and nurses were segregated in the army and an all-Negro hospital was established at Fort Huachuca in 1942. The army had for some time maintained a policy of nonsegregated treatment for patients, and Negro pressure groups, William H. Hastie in the War Department, Eleanor Roosevelt, and some congressmen joined to advocate the wider use of Negro physicians and nurses and desegregation for them as well. As a result, the number of Negro nurses in the army increased from 218 in December 1943 to 512 in July 1945. Many worked in segregated hospitals, but others were assigned to general hospitals and station hospitals in the United States, and there was less segregation at war's end. During the conflict, the army activated several all-Negro hospital units, and Negro nurses served in the South Pacific, Africa, and Europe.[15]

Negro women served in largest numbers in the Women's Army Corps. Like the rest of the army, this corps was directed to fill 10.6 percent of its enrollment with Negroes. Observers interested in Negro rights kept watch on the status and well-being of women in the army. Mary McLeod Bethune requested that a Negro lawyer meet and interview Negro women officer candidates at the training school in Des Moines, Iowa, to determine if they had experienced racial discrimination.[16] It was determined that Negro candidates received the same treatment as their white peers, and a *Pittsburgh Courier* reporter so informed General Marshall.

Despite these favorable accounts, segregation was practiced against Negro WACs and other Negroes in the army. The NAACP protested the continued use of separate barracks, separate tables in mess halls, and different hours for use of swimming pools in training schools. The YWCA and the National Urban League also protested and WAC authorities referred the protests to the War Department. The pressure paid off in November 1942, when the War Department merged officer housing and messing at Fort Des Moines and desegregated other facilities. Segregationists objected to the War Department's action and asserted that recruit-

---

14 Roy Wilkins, "Nurses Go to War," *Crisis* 50 (February 1943): 42–43.

15 Clarence McKittrick Smith, *The Medical Department: Hospitalization and Evacuation, Zone of Interior,* The United States Army in World War II: The Technical Services (Washington, D.C.: Office of the Chief of Military History, Department of the Army, 1956), pp. 110–12.

16 Holt, *Mary McLeod Bethune,* p. 235.

ment of white women would drop. Yet, the recruitment of well-qualified Negro women was improved by the move.[17]

Despite the growing number of Negro recruits, the Women's Army Corps found that too many of them were in the lowest AGCT grades. For example, 66 percent of the Negro WAC recruits in May 1943 were in Grades IV and V, and only 6 percent were in Grade I compared to the 43 percent of whites in Grade I.[18] The situation became serious after their initial training, when the women went into the field and the corps found that its table of organization could support only a few people in the lowest grades. The creation of a new table of organization which included large numbers of menial workers would be viewed as discriminatory. The army tried to provide special training, which was generally unsuccessful, since most recruits could not pass. The army then shipped Negro WACs to stations whether they were needed or not, and this action merely shifted the problem to individual stations. The army never found a way to use unskilled and untrainable individuals regardless of color or race.

WACs in the higher AGCT grades generally performed well in their assigned tasks, including secretarial work, teaching arts and crafts in recreational therapy, postal service, laboratory work, and other technical duties. Negro WAC officers were assigned as troop officers and served in operational billets, especially in the quartermaster corps.

More qualified Negro women applied for enlistment by 1944 but there were still not enough to reach the desired racial quota within the WAC organization. One-fourth of the Negro recruits had clerical and professional skills compared to one-half of the white recruits. About 30 percent (compared to 34 percent of the whites) had experience in skilled or unskilled trades. These averages were much higher than those of Negro women in industry, yet the Women's Army Corps never reached the goal of 10.6 percent Negro women. The maximum was reached in 1945, when 4 percent of the corps, approximately 4,000, were Negroes.[19]

Negro WAC units had internal problems, and frequently dissension occurred in Grades IV and V. Negro officers had to deal with dissatisfied individuals and cope with loneliness on small stations, especially when there was only one Negro WAC officer

17 Mattie E. Treadwell, *The Women's Army Corps,* The United States Army in World War II: Special Studies (Washington, D.C.: Office of the Chief of Military History, Department of the Army, 1954), pp. 589–601, is the best summary of the Negro WACs.

18 Treadwell, *Women's Army Corps,* p. 593.

19 Treadwell, *Women's Army Corps,* p. 596.

assigned. Well-intentioned outside groups tended to see every problem as a matter of racial discrimination even when the problems of Negro WACs were identical to those confronting white WACs.

Negro WACs were ordered to the European theater primarily in response to pressure from well-wishers desiring them to have the same opportunities as white WACs. A Negro central postal battalion arrived in Europe in February 1945, and 40 percent were unskilled workers. White WAC units in the theater had only 1 percent unskilled personnel. Negro units were further handicapped because 40 percent of their personnel were in Grades IV and V of the AGCT scores—only 10 percent of the white units were so handicapped. Consequently, the performance of the Negro unit was below standard; it was affected by internal differences, and the members of the unit allegedly allowed mail to pile up unnecessarily. The army refused to send Negro WACs to the Pacific despite public pressure. Army officials justified their action by noting that commanders in the Pacific theater had not requested Negro units. A Women's Army Corps historian reported that[20]

> Training center authorities were inclined to wonder if the nuisance value of the constant civilian searching parties had not outweighed the military contributions of the women. In the field, comments of post commanders applied to ability rather than race: every skilled WAC was assignable regardless of race, and unskilled ones were never wanted.

The navy began recruitment of women late and thus did not set racial quotas or accept unqualified applicants. Its enrollments were restricted to a few and its interracial units were desegregated from the start. Negro pressure groups criticized the navy policy of refusing to accept Negro women, but after the policy was changed the pressure groups were more sympathetic toward the navy than toward the army regarding the enlistment of Negro women.[21]

---

20 Treadwell, *Women's Army Corps,* p. 601.

21 The NAACP issued a press release applauding the admission of Negro women as WAVEs and urged the coast guard and marines to admit women on a nonsegregated basis also. When Secretary Walter White reported to a board meeting of the directors of the NAACP that Negro women in training as WAVE officers would not be segregated but that enlisted women would, the board voted to protest the segregation of the latter. NAACP Board of Directors Minutes, November 13, 1944, p. 2. In NAACP Files, Series A, Box 12. For material on Negro WAVEs, see *Opportunity* 23 (January–March 1945): 40; *Monthly Summary* 2:4 (November 1944): 99; and 2:8 (March 1945): 216, 224.

CHAPTER 9

Double V

"V FOR VICTORY" was a popular wartime slogan, and Negroes soon advocated a "Double V" symbolizing victory at home as well as abroad.[1] Negroes generally supported the goal of victory against Germany and Japan, but they were ambivalent regarding the struggle for racial equality. Some felt that the issue should be dropped, or subordinated, to concentrate on the all-out effort to defeat the Axis Powers. The Negro leaders, however, were adamant. Negroes would fight for victory on both fronts at the same time. The first editorial published in *Crisis* after the U.S. entry into the war declared: "Now Is The Time Not To Be Silent." The editor reaffirmed the loyalty of Negro Americans, and he contended that the sacrifices should be for a

> new world which not only shall not contain a Hitler, but no Hitlerism. And to thirteen millions of American Negroes that means a fight for a world in which lynching, brutality, terror, humiliation and degradation through segregation and discrimination, shall have no place—either here or there.[2]

Negro leaders repeatedly spelled out what they meant by victory at home, and the book, *What the Negro Wants*, published in 1944, articulated their goals. The collected essays were written by fourteen prominent Negroes, and the editor, Rayford W. Logan, a professor of history at Howard University, explained that racial tensions required a "definition of terms and a clarification of issues by competent Negroes representing various shades of opin-

---

[1] For an example of the use of the term, see R. W. Gully to NAACP National Committee, June 15, 1944. In NAACP Files, 1944 (283:2). Gully, president of a Michigan branch of the NAACP, concludes his letter with the words: "Yours for Double Victory." The National Urban League summarized its work for 1941 under two general objectives: "(1) To Promote Effective Participation of Negroes in all phases of the war effort—military, naval, industrial and civilian. (2) To Formulate Plans for building the kind of United States in which we wish to live after the war is over and we have finally 'won the Peace'." "A Summary of the Activities of the National Urban League, January 1 to December 31, 1941." In Brotherhood of Sleeping Car Porters Records, Container No. 21. The *Pittsburgh Courier* started a "Double V" campaign; and in its May 12, 1942, meeting the NAACP Board of Directors voted to support the campaign. NAACP Board of Directors Minutes, May 12, 1942, p. 5. In NAACP Files, Series A, Box 11.

[2] *Crisis* 49 (January 1942): 7 (editorial).

ion." Logan wrote one of the articles and selected the other contributors, "four of whom might be called conservatives, five liberals, and five radicals." The editor noted that there was "surprising unanimity with respect to what the Negro wants. Conservatives, liberals, and radicals alike want the Negroes eventually to enjoy the same rights, opportunities and privileges that are vouchsafed to all other Americans and to fulfill all the obligations that are required of all other Americans."[3]

Negroes tried to win the war at home in different ways. Many felt that the fight for equality could be won by demonstrating the Negro's worth as full fighting partners in the war. Thus, many Negroes willingly left their customary ways of life and, to the extent that they were permitted, did their share in the war against the Axis. Negroes worked in war plants, served in the armed services, worked in government, toured military camps to build morale and sell war bonds, served as war correspondents, and performed other wartime duties. Many Negroes, especially those connected with pressure groups, approved these efforts and resented actions that prevented them from contributing their full share. Most favored an assault against the enemies of domestic democracy.

Negroes often appealed directly to the sense of fair play of other Americans. A student at Princeton University emphasized that approach: "You can discriminate against me because I'm uncouth and I can become mannerly. You can ostracize me because I'm unclean and I can cleanse myself. You can segregate me because I'm ignorant and I can become learned; but if you hate me because of my color, I can do nothing; God gave me that."[4] Other Negroes noted the discrepancies between nationally announced war aims and conditions in the United States, again in an appeal to fair play. Negroes often employed sarcasm and irony, and *Crisis,* for example, commented on the report that whites proposed constructing segregated bomb shelters in Washington, D.C.: "Wouldn't it be just like Hitler to make American whites choose a 'fate worse than death'—running into a Negro bomb shelter?"[5] *Opportunity* noted that southern whites paradoxically extolled the virtues of the Negro "Mammy," while the

---

3 Rayford W. Logan, ed., *What the Negro Wants* (Chapel Hill: University of North Carolina Press, 1944). The quotations are from the preface, pp. vii–viii.

4 As quoted in *Monthly Summary of Events and Trends in Race Relations* 1:8 (April 1944): 27.

5 *Crisis* 49 (January 1942): 7 (editorial).

War Department refused to accept Negro nurses for service except "in hospitals or wards devoted exclusively to the treatment of Negro soldiers."[6] Langston Hughes wrote, "To a southbound Negro citizen told in Washington to change into a segregated coach, the *Four Freedoms* have a hollow sound."[7]

Sarcasm occasionally became bitter. Negroes resented the American Red Cross decision to segregate blood donated by Negroes and whites and cited experts to prove that the scientific separation of blood was based on individual blood types or groups and not on race. They emphasized that one of the ablest scientific experts on blood plasma was a Negro. Dr. Charles R. Drew, head of the Department of Surgery, School of Medicine, Howard University, explained:[8]

> When a blood transfusion is given, the donor's blood must be compatible with that of the recipient, that is, Group or Type A blood from an individual of any race would be suitable for transfusion into the veins of an individual of any race providing it is blood of the same group. . . . The necessity for typing blood was made unnecessary by removing the cells from all bloods and pooling the plasma. This process makes the final product suitable for infusion into the blood stream of any blood group. . . . The whole question of race of donors is a social one and must be put in the same category as jim crowism, restricted residential sections, and job allocations on the basis of race.

The American Red Cross steadfastly refused to alter its policy, which it blamed on army and navy leaders. The Red Cross *Bulletin* published a Policy Regarding Negro Donors which stated that the Red Cross accepted Negro blood and processed it separately "so that those receiving transfusions may be given plasma from blood of their own race." The *Bulletin* asserted that no official connected with the donor project had ever stated that there was "any evidence that the blood of negroes [sic] differs in any respect from that of white persons." The *Bulletin* continued, "In spite of this fact there are many persons who have a deep-rooted senti-

6 *Opportunity* 20 (February 1942): 34 (editorial).

7 As quoted in *Monthly Summary* 1:5 (December 1943): 30.

8 Charles R. Drew to Warren M. Banner, Director of Research, National Urban League, New York, January 9, 1942. In National Urban League Files, Series VI, Box 9. In 1943, the NAACP decided not to support the American Red Cross fund-raising drives because of the blood donor policy. See NAACP Board of Directors Minutes, March 8, 1943, p. 2. In NAACP Files, Series A, Box 12.

ment against the indiscriminate mixing of white and Negro blood into the preparation of plasma to be used for blood transfusions." It claimed that unfortunately, the differences of opinion on the mixing of blood were too great to be reconciled. Therefore, there was "no alternative but to recognize the existence of a point of view, the disregarding of which might militate against the present successful conduct of the blood plasma project.[9] Basil O'Connor succeeded Norman Davis as president of the American Red Cross and in the summer of 1944, the NAACP tried to persuade O'Connor to change the policy. He declined, stating that he was convinced that the existing policy was the "best possible in all of the circumstances."[10] Negro bitterness surfaced for a variety of reasons. Grant Reynolds, a former chaplain, wrote three articles for *Crisis* (1944) elaborating his thesis that Negro soldiers had been "sold a rotten bill of goods." Dr. Lewis K. McMillan, a professor at Wilberforce University, suggested that Reynolds had missed the real issue, which was the underlying causes of Jim Crowism. McMillan wrote, "The tragedy in Reynolds' case is that he is so personally hurt over bitter experiences of racial prejudice encountered in army camps and elsewhere that he has closed his eyes to basic evils which breed racial prejudice and all the other social evils."[11]

The Negro press hammered away at Jim Crowism and discrimination. The news stories centered on matters which created the greatest tensions, including public transportation, housing, education, military service, and the views of southern white extremists. Some accounts emphasized the physical or legal punishments imposed on Negroes while others depicted Negroes standing up for their rights through physical actions or in the courts. Some cited cases of Negroes resorting to violence—Negro men using knives in fights. A Negro woman reportedly threw a white woman conductor through a streetcar window after the conductor had hit her with a metal crank. The violence, cited mostly in the Negro press, involved white civilians and police. Although such incidents were isolated, most reflected the current tensions and the possibility of mass disorder, the increasing rejection of discrimina-

---

[9] A copy of the bulletin is enclosed with letter, Luther L. Barlow, Chairman Plainfield and North Plainfield Chapter, American Red Cross, to Anne Mather, National Urban League, March 27, 1944. In National Urban League Files, Series VI, Box 9.

[10] NAACP Board of Directors Minutes, September 11, 1944, p. 2. In NAACP Files, Series A, Box 12.

[11] Cited in *Crisis* 52 (January 1945): 28.

tion by Negroes, and the refusal of racist whites to accept social change.

During World War II few Negro entertainers injected social messages into their performances. Guitarist and singer Josh White was an exception. He broadcast weekly from New York, was a frequent guest on other shows, made records, and contributed programs for the Office of War Information. He also performed in person at Barney Josefson's Cafe Society at Sheridan Square. White's act switched from popular numbers to such songs as "Jim Crow Train." One journalist described the singer in these words: "Josh White ceases to be merely an entertainer. He is a voice of protest, in an uncamouflaged set-to with the forces of his nation which keep him and the members of his race second-class citizens. On the faces turned in his direction is a mingling of amazement, uneasiness, admiration, and sometimes a fierce resentment." Some of his audience walked out, but White said, "I can't stop on account of that." White's songs also eulogized Dorie Miller, Negro hero of Pearl Harbor, lamented the hard work of Negroes in southern fields and Jim Crowism in the air forces, and included a "Bad Housing Wail" and the "Defense Factory Blues."

Negroes often acted jointly against racial discrimination. Their violent reactions were examined earlier, and nonviolent responses are worth noting as portents. First, Negroes and whites alike employed picketing in response to labor disputes. Negroes and whites joined in picketing a theater in Washington, D.C., in February 1940. The pickets carried placards which urged, "Don't patronize this theater, Negroes cannot enter." But the effort was not noticeably successful. *Opportunity* published an editorial which pointed out that the picture being shown was the premiere of *Abraham Lincoln in Illinois*. The editorial further observed, "There were four members in the cabinet in that brilliant company who crossed the picket line, three judges of the Supreme Court, and the wife of the President of the United States of America."[12]

The second nonviolent protest technique employed by Negroes was an early prototype of the sit-ins popularized during the 1960s. Howard University was a natural setting for Negro discontent, since the students had experienced discrimination in all parts of the country. Students from northern and northwestern states chafed at the evidence of racial discrimination they found in and around Washington, D.C. Three Negro women students entered

---

[12] *Opportunity* 18 (February 1940): 34–35 (editorial).

a United Cigar store early in 1943 and demanded to see the manager when the waitress refused to serve them hot chocolate.[13] The manager approved serving them but they were overcharged. The students paid the amount customarily charged for such drinks and were subsequently arrested and spent the night in jail. Howard University administrators urged the three students to forget the incident but they refused and were joined by other students. One of them, William Raines, a law student, had been promoting what he called the "stool-sitting technique" based on the notion that "if the white people want to deny us service, let them pay for it." Raines encouraged students to occupy seats in restaurants during rush hours and just sit reading books. He reasoned that the establishments would lose business and thus change their policy. A woman student from Boston had already tried the system with some success. The students formed a committee and circulated a questionnaire to the student body in February 1943. Some 292 out of a total enrollment of 2,000 replied, and 97.3 percent of the respondents stated that Negroes should not suspend working for civil rights during the war. The same proportion indicated that students should participate actively in a struggle for civil rights, and a majority stated they would participate.

The result of their survey encouraged the students to form a civil rights committee sponsored by the student chapter of the NAACP. The committee then formed subcommittees to work for the passage of civil rights bills which had been introduced in Congress. In addition, another subcommittee was formed to practice the "stool-sitting technique," which was combined with what the students called a "sit-it-out-in-your-most-dignified-bib-and-tucker." The students first concentrated on the Little Palace Cafeteria, in the heart of a Negro section, run by a Greek-American who would not accept Negro trade. The group prepared by carefully studying the antipicketing and disorderly conduct laws of Washington and confirmed their decision to maintain peaceful conduct. The students made their move on a rainy Saturday afternoon in April, entering the cafeteria in groups of three and keeping a fourth member outside as a lookout. After being refused service the students remained in their seats to read or write letters. Other groups entered and the students soon occupied half the seats. The management closed the establishment less than an hour later, and the students remained outside picketing with signs, one of which

---

13 Details of this incident are taken largely from Pauli Murray, "A Blueprint for First Class Citizenship," *Crisis* 51 (November 1944): 358-59.

stated, "We Die Together—Why Can't We Eat Together?" After two days of being picketed, the management changed its policy.

The elated subcommittee then tried bigger game, Thompson's Cafeteria at Fourteenth Street and Pennsylvania Avenue, near the White House. Students again moved on a Saturday afternoon and filled half the seats in the cafeteria. The local manager called the main office in Chicago and was ordered to serve the Negroes. The students then sought to negotiate a permanent change in policy but were blocked by Howard University officials. The university deans and other administrators directed the students to stop all activities "designed to accomplish social reform affecting institutions other than Howard University itself." The disappointed students then abandoned social action to seek a student-faculty-administrative committee empowered to make recommendations on student affairs. The students found in the process that 60 percent of the university's financial support came from the federal government and that some congressmen would seek to cut or eliminate those funds whenever budgets were discussed. That finding may have explained the conservative attitude of the university's administration.

Many Negroes, including the top leaders, enlisted the support of whites to work with them to further democracy at home. The NAACP and the National Urban League sought the cooperation of other groups. One important journal was the *Monthly Summary of Events and Trends in Race Relations,* which began publication in August 1943 and which emphasized the joint efforts of interracial groups. The journal, sponsored by the Julius Rosenwald Fund, was prepared by the Social Science Institute at Fisk University, under the direction of Charles S. Johnson, a prominent Negro scholar. One section of the publication, "Programs of Action on the Democratic Front," reported in the first issue that the National Education Association had resolved not to meet in cities where full accommodations were not available for all. The report also cited a conference sponsored by the Baltimore Urban League attended by 100 Negro and white citizens to consider racial tensions, a rally attended by 20,000 Negroes and whites in Madison Square Garden in New York on June 7, 1943, and a meeting of Negro leaders with the mayor of Cincinnati in which they recommended ways to reduce racial tension.[14]

The organization of the Southern Regional Council resulted

---

14 *Monthly Summary* 1:1 (August 1943): 16–18.

from a series of biracial meetings. The council included fourteen Negro and sixteen white members temporarily cochaired by Professor Howard W. Odum of the University of North Carolina and Professor Charles S. Johnson of Fisk University. The council proposed to support and strengthen the FEPC, support passage of the anti-poll-tax bill, call a conference of mayors and governors to "prepare a program for protecting Negroes in local situations of police and court injustice, and organize citizens' committees in every locality." The council's proposals were moderate; for instance, it did not advocate immediate desegregation of the armed forces. Rather, it recommended the establishment of "experimental mixed units of volunteers in the Army and Navy." The council explained that "no one need be forced into them. But there are plenty of Americans, white and black, who want to give democracy a chance in the armed forces."[15]

The Chicago mayor's Committee on Race Relations, led by Edwin R. Embree, president of the Julius Rosenwald Fund and a prominent white worker for interracial cooperation, became one of the most active local committees. The committee announced that it would gather information on broad and definite issues, make recommendations to the mayor and appropriate agencies, encourage construction programs, and support popular education on interracial relations. The *Monthly Summary of Events and Trends in Race Relations* reported in November 1943 that the Chicago committee's "recommendations to the police department and to the Mayor carry sufficient weight to receive not only attention but action."[16] Robert C. Weaver, chief of Minority Group Services, War Manpower Commission, was appointed as codirector of the mayor's committee early in 1944 as a "professionally trained and experienced expert," to administer the committee's program.[17] As part of its continuing work, the committee sponsored a conference in May and June 1945 and the Dumbarton Oaks Plan for Chicago emerged. The plan created commissions on employment, housing, education, law and order, recreation,

---

15 *Monthly Summary* 1:1 (August 1943): 18–19. Walter White's comments on this conference annoyed P. B. Young of the *Norfolk Journal and Guide* and he wrote to White: "Although you do not seem to think so, southern Negro Leaders do think for themselves and do plan actions which they consider in their best interests without consulting New York. . . . It seems to me you would have been as considerate of the Durham conferees as they were of you and numerous other leaders who live in the north. . . ." Young to White, February 27, 1943. In NAACP Files, 1943 (291:2).

16 *Monthly Summary* 1:4 (November 1943): 13, 20.

17 *Monthly Summary* 1:6 (January 1944): 13.

and health and welfare to work for racial harmony, fight bigotry and hatred, and promote peace.

Codirector Embree called a conference of seventy-one leading Negroes and whites to meet in Chicago in March 1944. The NAACP leaders were unsympathetic. Roy Wilkins was mildly critical of the meeting in his report to the NAACP board of directors,[18] and Walter White wrote Dr. Louis T. Wright to express acute dissatisfaction with the council's leadership.[19] The *Journal and Globe* in Norfolk reported (April 1, 1944) that "if any proof was needed that the American Race problem had become national in scope it was furnished by the Conference on Race Relations held in Chicago, March 21–22," and the editor concluded that "on the whole the conference was illuminating."[20] After the March conference the American Council on Race Relations was created; a second meeting in May 1944 led to the announcement of a five-point program. The new council proposed to research and disseminate information about race relations, assist local committees, and use mass communications to increase popular understanding of race relations. Negro leaders Will Alexander, Lester B. Granger, Charles S. Johnson, Robert C. Weaver, Walter White, and prominent whites attended the May meeting. The council established its headquarters in Chicago and a regional office in San Francisco.

A few interracial committees subsequently appeared in the South and in other parts of the country but their announced aims were usually much more modest. The Unity for Victory Committee was formed in Baltimore as an outgrowth of the earlier committee organized by the National Urban League for the prevention and control of riots. A biracial committee of twelve was established in Charleston, South Carolina, "to investigate all reports of unrest, attempt to remove misunderstandings, and promote a better spirit of cooperation between the races."[21]

The governor of Illinois in response to the recommendation of a statewide commission asked fourteen downstate cities with large Negro populations to establish local interracial committees. The National Urban League urged its local chapters to confer with city officials, business and labor leaders, and other elements of the community to prevent riots. Fisk University, in Nashville,

---

18 Report to board by Wilkins, April 4, 1944. In NAACP Files, 1944 (291:5).
19 Walter White to Dr. Louis T. Wright. In NAACP Files 1944 (291:5).
20 Clipping. In NAACP Files, 1944 (291:5).
21 *Monthly Summary* 1:2 (September 1943): 18.

sponsored an institute in the summer of 1944 to improve race relations. Well-known Negroes Charles S. Johnson, Robert C.
Weaver, Willard Townsend, Will Alexander, and Lester B.
Granger participated as seminar leaders. This successful institute
led to others throughout the country—an interracial workshop in
Berkeley, the Harvard Workshop on Race, a statewide race relations conference in Durham, North Carolina, and a seminar on
race and culture at Western Reserve University in Ohio.

The *Monthly Summary of Events and Trends in Race Relations* reported the growth of interracial committees and noted that
there were 224 such organizations. The *Monthly Summary* listed
166 of those committees, 15 national, 16 state, and 135 local.[22]
The local committees resulted from the efforts of citizens; most
of the state organizations were created by officials. The committees often included other minorities, and Negro leaders consis-
tently sympathized with the Japanese-Americans in relocation
centers and expressed interest in reducing anti-Semitism among
Negroes in some of the larger northern cities. Some of the local
committees reflected religious orientations, others represented
labor interests, especially the CIO, and still others appealed
mainly to youths.

The Movie Committee for Mass Education in Race Relations,
supported by the American Film Center, Hollywood Writers'
Mobilization, the Julius Rosenwald Fund, the NAACP, and the
American Council on Race Relations, was formed to enhance
democratic action. The committee included Langston Hughes,
Countee Cullen, the ubiquitous Charles S. Johnson, and Ira De
A. Reid. Many leaders of the literary and theatrical world served
as consultants, among them John Dos Passos, Carey McWilliams,
Walter Wanger, Josh White, and Orson Welles. The *Monthly
Summary* reported that the committee planned a "frontal attack
on racial problems through the medium of motion pictures telling
the stories of racial minorities in the United States." Several
scripts, including *The Negro Speaks of Rivers,* a narration by
Langston Hughes about the Negro "from his African heritage to
the present," had already been completed.[23]

The growing effort to better human relations began to attract
national publicity. February 1945 was proclaimed Brotherhood

22 *Monthly Summary* 2:1–2 (August–September 1944): 24–32. For other
organizations, see listing of 138 committees in enclosure of letter from Eliza-
beth Allan, Julius Rosenwald Fund, to Walter White, June 22, 1944. In
NAACP Files, 1944 (291:4).

23 *Monthly Summary* 2:7 (February 1945): 201–2.

Month, and churches participated by celebrating Race Relations Sunday and by sponsoring brotherhood meetings. Fifty-seven cities recognized Negro History Week through various programs and exhibits; for example, Mayor La Guardia proclaimed February 12–18, 1945, to be Negro History Week.

The *Monthly Summary* in its April 1945 issue noted one shortcoming of the interracial committee movement—Negroes served on those committees as representatives of the Negro group and not as members of the community. The *Monthly Summary* cited several instances of the broader representation and noted that it was a necessary step forward.[24]

Certain Negro leaders took a stand of their own as the election of 1944 drew near. They advocated a "Negro Bill of Rights" supported by twenty-five national Negro groups as both a statement of objectives and a warning. The proposed bill supported making the Committee on Fair Employment Practice permanent, ending segregation in the armed forces, and including Negroes in the U.S. Peace Conference delegations. The bill further asserted:[25]

> We hereby serve notice that if either major political party shall nominate for President or Vice-President a candidate of vacillating or reactionary character or with an anti-Negro record, it will be vigorously opposed by Negro voters. We repudiate all such persons, Negro or white, who attempt for personal profit to "deliver the Negro vote."

The bill of rights was designed by A. Philip Randolph, William H. Hastie, Thurgood Marshall, Walter White, Roy Wilkins, and Adam Clayton Powell, Jr.

The bill was prepared at a conference of Negro leaders held in New York, on June 17, 1944, organized by Walter White. White later wrote to A. Philip Randolph, who did not attend, that there was remarkable agreement among the conferees. That unity resulted in the selection of a committee to appear at the party conventions to represent all the twenty-five organizations. White wrote, "We all felt that this demonstration of unity would have an effect upon the political parties, upon the Country as a whole, and upon Negro opinion. . . ."[26] White responded to a question

---

24 *Monthly Summary* 2:9 (April 1945): 269–71.
25 Cited in *Monthly Summary* 1:11 (July 1944): 16.
26 White to Randolph, June 19, 1944. In NAACP Files, 1945 (359:1).

concerning why whites had not been invited to attend: "It has been thought wise to confine attendance at the meeting on June 17th to Negroes speaking on behalf of Negroes from a non-partisan, non-political, non-sectional point of view expressing on behalf of Negroes what he expects of political parties." He added, "We are not calling a color line against white people but, as I stated before, it has been thought best to confine the meeting to Negroes."[27]

During the summer of 1943 the Congress of Racial Equality (CORE) grew out of local committees for racial equality. CORE was dedicated to "working to abolish racial discrimination by direct, non-violent methods,"[28] and little was heard of it until 1945. Then, headed by James L. Farmer, field representative for the Fellowship of Reconciliation,[29] CORE announced its Summer Non-Violent Direct Action Campaign to Help Uproot Jim Crowism in an American Community, which was planned to last from June 18 to August 18, 1945, and to involve training volunteers in Chicago. The campaign was described as follows:[30]

> The action will consist of investigating areas of racial tension, negotiating problems discovered with those who are officially responsible, and taking further action such as distributing leaflets, picketing, etc., if the situation demands this.

The vigorous interracial actions of the Chicago mayor's committee and the war's end probably prevented CORE from gaining much early attention. Even the Negro journals failed to play up the proposed campaign.

Negroes and others interested in racial equality also sought victory at home by continuing to fight in the courts for their civil rights. The *Classic* case, discussed in Chapter 1, led to invalidation

---

27 White to P. B. Young, June 13, 1944. In NAACP Files, 1945 (359:1).

28 *Monthly Summary* 1:1 (August 1943): 16.

29 In 1943, Ray W. Gould, an attorney from Cambridge, Massachusetts, sent Walter White an appraisal of the Fellowship of Reconciliation, which in conjunction with the March on Washington had held an institute in Boston, March 26–28, 1943. Gould wrote that the most active members of FOR were also members of the Socialist Party. Their activities were mainly with Japanese in relocation camps and with conscientious objectors. He termed FOR, which claimed a membership of 200 in the Boston area, mainly a pacifist outfit. He added, "O, yes, the staff of FOR feel that the NAACP cannot do effective work because 'it cannot head a mass movement for the top officers make direct decisions and the mass of negro [sic] members just pay one dollar membership fee as an obligation and follow the direction of leaders.'" Ray W. Gould to Walter White, April 5, 1943. In NAACP Files, 1943 (270:3).

30 *Monthly Summary* 2:10 (May 1945): 297.

of the white primary, the most formidable barrier to Negro voting rights. The *Classic* decision upheld the power of Congress to regulate state primary congressional elections and the contention that the primary is an integral part of the election process. The Supreme Court declared the white primary unconstitutional in *Smith v. Allwright* (1944). Justice Stanley Reed speaking for the eight-to-one majority said, "It may be taken as a postulate that the right to vote in such a primary for the nomination of candidates without discrimination by the State, like the right to vote in a general election, is a right secured by the Constitution."[31] The decision resulted in protest throughout the South, but people in the border states tended to accept the decision. Southern states with large Negro populations responded with diehard delaying actions. Mississippi, Alabama, and South Carolina passed legislation designed to circumvent the Court's decision. South Carolina's plan to retain the white primary was checked by a hard-hitting U.S. district judge, who advised: "It is time for South Carolina to rejoin the Union. It is time to fall in step with the other states and to adopt the American way of conducting elections."[32] The Supreme Court's decision was clear, but it took time to implement it in the Deep South.

Negro civil rights were further advanced when Georgia abolished the poll tax in 1945. The editor of *Crisis* was encouraged enough to write that if the Negro could obtain the ballot "he and the South" could "go a long way toward solving some of their problems." The editor predicted the average Negro voter would prove to be "no better and certainly no worse than whites," and he prophesied that some would "sell their votes for cash or favors just as do whites. Some will vote for the good of the whole community and some for their own selfish interests."[33] Seven southern states retained the poll tax; however, the real obstacle to the Negro's exercise of the franchise was the white primary.

The efforts of the Civil Rights Section of the Criminal Division of the Department of Justice were noted in Chapter 1. This unit continually produced gains beneficial to the Negro throughout

---

31 On the basis of this decision, Thurgood Marshall urged the attorney general "to issue definite instructions" to all United States attorneys to take action in the case of "refusal to permit qualified Negro electors to vote in primary elections" in the states affected. Thurgood Marshall, Special Counsel, NAACP Legal Defense and Educational Fund, Inc., to Francis J. Biddle, Attorney General, April 3, 1944. In NAACP Files, 1944 (285:2).

32 As quoted in V. O. Key, Jr., *Southern Politics in State and Nation* (New York: Alfred A. Knopf, 1949), p. 628.

33 *Crisis* 52 (March 1945): 73 (editorial).

the war. The efforts of the Civil Rights Section are best exemplified by its involvement in *Screws v. United States* (1945). The case involved "one of the most serious threats to civil liberties" and "the contempt of many local law enforcement officers for the rights of weak and helpless members of minority groups." Claude Screws, sheriff of Baker County, Georgia, arrested a Negro, Robert Hall, on a warrant charging tire theft in January 1943. Screws and two other police officers assaulted Hall and on arrival at the police station threw him on the jail floor. Hall was taken to a hospital, where he died without regaining consciousness. The incident was reported to the Civil Rights Section, which tried unsuccessfully to persuade the state of Georgia to institute charges. Georgia officials believed that prosecution was up to local authorities, who refused to act. The U.S. attorney, assisted by a lawyer from the Civil Rights Section, presented the case to a federal grand jury, which returned an indictment against Screws and the two police officers on charges of violating Section 52 of the United States Code. The defendants were brought to trial, but the Civil Rights Section lost the legal battle because the accused were acquitted in two trials. Despite loss of the legal battle, Robert K. Carr noted, "The basic constitutionality of Section 52, as used in a police brutality case to protect the right to due process of law, was upheld."[34] The *Screws* case was thus a disappointingly short but nevertheless important step forward in the cause of civil liberties.

Negroes also made substantial gains in their struggle for equality of opportunity in federal employment during the war. Several factors contributed to their success, but the wartime shortage of labor was the most important. Negro pressure groups continued to demand equality of opportunity, and President Roosevelt's Executive Order 8802, followed by letters to department heads, was also influential. The Committee on Fair Employment Practice stimulated the employment of minority workers in federal jobs and in industry. The Ramspeck Act of 1940 barred discrimination in federal employment, and the Civil Service Commission helped encourage the employment of Negroes.

The greatest increase in federal employment occurred in Washington, D.C., and the number of Negroes employed rose from 80,000 in 1938 to about 300,000 in 1944, an increase of from 9.8 to 11.9 percent of the labor force. Most Negro workers were in unskilled positions because of continued discrimination in spite

---

[34] Robert K. Carr, *Federal Protection of Civil Rights: Quest for a Sword* (Ithaca, N.Y.: Cornell University Press, 1947), p. 113.

of the regulations and because of their generally lower educational qualifications.[35] Some Negroes, however, were employed in higher-level positions and many of them remained in those positions after the war. Samuel Krislov noted, "There was no repetition of the post-World War I situation where Negro gains were wiped out almost overnight."[36]

The status of Negroes was significantly enhanced because of the public recognition given to individuals. There was undoubtedly an element of tokenism in these honors but that tokenism was considered necessary and represented an advance in itself. For example, merchant vessels (Liberty ships) built during the war were named in honor of prominent Americans. Several were named for Negroes and the first, not surprisingly, honored Booker T. Washington. Marian Anderson christened the vessel and sang "The Star-spangled Banner," and Mary McLeod Bethune delivered the dedication address.[37] A second Liberty ship was named in honor of the Negro scientist George Washington Carver and launched in Richmond, California, in May 1943. The ship was christened by singer Lena Horne, who toured the shipyards after the christening and sold $25,000 in war bonds.[38] Other Liberty ships were named in honor of John Hope, former president of Atlanta University; James Weldon Johnson, the first executive secretary of the NAACP; and Robert S. Abbott, founder and long-time editor of the *Chicago Defender*.[39] The *Marine Eagle* was the first warship to be built entirely by Negroes and it was launched by the Sun Shipbuilding and Drydock Company of Chester, Pennsylvania. The *Marine Eagle* was sponsored by Rachel Stevenson, who was employed as a cleaner in the office of the company president and who was given a corsage and a $1,000 war bond.[40]

Living Negroes received honors and recognition in greater numbers during World War II than ever before. Marian Anderson received an honorary Doctor of Music degree from Smith College in 1944. In the same year E. Franklin Frazier, professor of sociol-

---

35 For discussions of this matter, see Paul P. Van Riper, *History of the United States Civil Service* (Evanston: Row, Peterson, 1958), pp. 378–79; Gladys M. Kammerer, *Impact of War on Federal Personnel Administration* (Lexington: University of Kentucky Press, 1951), pp. 50–55.

36 Samuel Krislov, *The Negro in Federal Employment: The Quest for Equal Opportunity* (Minneapolis: University of Minnesota Press, 1967), p. 33.

37 *Opportunity* 20 (October 1942): 308.

38 *Opportunity* 21 (July 1943): 122.

39 *Monthly Summary* 1:6 (January 1944): 2.

40 *Opportunity* 21 (July 1943): 122.

ogy at Howard University, was elected president of the Eastern
Sociological Society, the first Negro "to be elected to the presidency of a scientific society with a mixed membership."[41] W. E.
B. DuBois was the first Negro to be elected to the National Institute of Arts and Letters. Earlier, in 1942, Dr. Kenneth Clark had
been appointed assistant professor at the College of the City of
New York, "the first Negro to be added to the regular faculty."[42]
Negro "firsts" occurred elsewhere during the war—the first Negro
member of a hospital staff, the first Negro attorney appointed to
a section in the Criminal Division of the Department of Justice,
the first Negro captain of a Liberty ship.

Langston Hughes wrote an article for *Crisis* entitled "Need
for Heroes" in June 1940. There were Negro heroes before
and during World War II, but they were specialized and none developed into national leaders. Negroes everywhere thrilled to Joe
Louis's exploits. Louis contributed to the war effort, and his visits
to military bases effectively increased national morale. Ironically,
Louis turned over his winnings from one fight to Navy Relief at
a time when the navy would accept Negro enlistees only as messmen. The countless acts of heroism by Negroes in the war seldom
received national attention, yet one was frequently mentioned in
the Negro press as an example of what Negroes could do if they
were permitted to fight. Dorie Miller received the Navy Cross for
bravery during the attack on Pearl Harbor. Miller, a messman,
was not trained for battle, yet he manned a machine gun on the
West Virginia to engage the attacking Japanese planes. Miller
was later reported missing at sea.[43]

The work of the men who directed the NAACP and the National Urban League was important, but they were not leaders in
a broad sense. Their organizations represented only the middle
class despite their announced goal of bettering the lot of Negroes
generally. The Negro masses lived in large cities and were leader-
less, and this is why Langston Hughes wrote of the need for heroes.
Hughes noted that history might later recall Negro representatives
remembered not as heroes but in effect as nonheroes or antiheroes.
Bigger Thomas, the principal figure in Richard Wright's *Native
Son*, published in 1940, was such an antihero. Bigger was a com-
posite of five persons whom Wright had observed, he was " 'the

41 *Monthly Summary* 1:10 (June 1944): 14.

42 *Opportunity* 20 (November 1942): 341.

43 Walter Karig and Wellbourn Kelley, *Battle Report: Pearl Harbor to
Coral Sea* (New York: Farrar & Rinehart, 1944), pp. 71, 73.

bad nigger' set down without squeamishness, doing all that the 'bad nigger' is supposed to do."[44] Wright's purpose was "to show that the individual's delinquency is produced by a distorting environment rather than by innate criminality."[45]

None of the Negro politicians prominent during the war showed signs of becoming a national leader. Their followings were local, and they lacked the opportunity to operate on the national scene. Adam Clayton Powell, Jr., possessed a potential for national leadership, but it was too early to see what course he would take. A. Philip Randolph certainly might be classed as a national Negro leader during the March on Washington. The Negro leadership would fight for victory at home but not at the expense of victory in the war against foreign enemies.

---

[44] *Opportunity* 18 (June 1940): 185.
[45] Hugh M. Gloster, "Richard Wright: Interpreter of Racial and Economic Maladjustments," *Opportunity* 19 (December 1941): 383.

CHAPTER 10

The Balance Sheet

WHAT WERE the basic changes in the status of the American Negro after the war? During the war, there had been a tremendous shifting among people in the United States. The movement of Negroes to the North accelerated greatly. Thousands moved to the West Coast, drawn by war industries and war duties. The shift of Negroes from agrarian to urban life was an important aspect of these movements. Many northern whites in the military witnessed conditions in the South which previously they had only read about. Even larger numbers of southern whites carried their ideas of race relationships to the North and West. The question of the Negro's place in society ceased to be mainly a southern concern and became a national issue. The character of race relationships in the South changed in the process.

The movement largely involved Negro men and women in uniform. The military leaders announced that their job was to prepare their forces to fight, not to solve social problems that had baffled civilians for years. The Negro made some gains despite the military's attitude. The military maintained a policy of segregation but the seeds of its destruction were planted and took root. The "Double V" symbolized the illogic of segregated armies' fighting a war for democracy. The war also proved that Negroes were effective in uniform and that equivalent educations and backgrounds enabled them to compete on a par with whites. Clearly, the war demonstrated that it was in the national interest to provide equivalent educations and backgrounds for Negroes. The integration of Negroes into the coast guard, on a few naval vessels, and on some military bases showed that it would work.

The struggle against segregation made little headway during the war, but the campaign against discrimination was advanced by the continued prodding by the Negro leaders and press. Some whites also opposed discrimination because it hampered the war effort and was inconsistent with the nation's democratic ideals. Military leaders thus tried to reduce the effects of discrimination by eliminating Jim Crow transportation and trying to treat Negroes in uniform the same as their white counterparts.

During the war significant gains were achieved in Negro civil rights. The war was not responsible directly for those gains, but it accelerated their accomplishment, since a nation could not question the need to extend those rights at home while fighting for them overseas. The most important single advance was the destruction of white primaries in the South. Military travel hastened the end of Jim Crow conditions in transportation. Finally, Negroes increasingly believed they could gain more from the federal government than from state and local governments.

The war years produced a few Negro spokesmen who had national significance. Bethune, for example, continued to exert influence at the federal level, especially in behalf of Negro women, and her opinions affected the enrollment of Negro women in the military forces. Walter White's visits to the major theaters of war set a precedent which enlightened Secretary of the Navy Forrestal. After the war Forrestal dispatched Lester B. Granger to U.S. naval facilities to study conditions. Granger made numerous recommendations to Forrestal.[1]

The most successful Negro leaders during the war worked for attainable practical goals. At the same time, they gave notice that they also sought long-range objectives. They pushed for democracy at home and abroad. The war in progress had overwhelming public support, so there was no significant disagreement among Negroes as to the ultimate objectives. *What the Negro Wants* included statements by Negro leaders which clearly noted that the similarities of their objectives were far more striking than their differences.

Generally speaking, leaders of both races cooperated in an effort to reduce discrimination and improve race relations and the wartime increase of interracial conferences and study groups attests to that cooperation. The war, however, failed to resolve the Negro's dilemma, whether to concentrate on achieving racial integration or a separate racial identity. The resulting ambivalence affected A. Philip Randolph, who sought to improve the lot of Negro workers by joining the white-controlled American Federation of Labor. Yet he spearheaded the projected March on Washington, and he insisted that the march be limited to Negroes. Randolph then joined other Negro leaders in drafting and publicizing a "Negro Bill of Rights" in 1944 in an attempt to pull together the Negro vote in the election of 1944. Whites were not invited to attend the meeting in which the bill was drafted.

Negroes made significant gains in the field of labor during the

---

[1] Lawrence D. Reddick, "The Negro in the United States Navy During World War II," *Journal of Negro History* 32 (April 1947): 215.

war. The gains reflected the needs of war production and a shortage of labor. Negro leaders feared that the last hired would be the first fired when the war ended. Despite this possibility, thousands of Negroes became skilled rather than unskilled workers through war training, and they received higher wages and the promise of a better standard of living. They found employment in fields which formerly excluded them. So many Negroes performed so effectively in government that they could not be removed from postwar employment on the basis of race alone. Finally the myth of Negro labor's inferiority was ended by the war. The war destroyed the assumption that Negro workers were strikebreakers, and the double standard of wages for the same kind of work was dealt a serious blow. The war opened jobs for women of both races and highlighted the need for an expansion of women's rights.

Despite the real gains achieved during World War II, progress appeared entirely too slow to many Negroes, who feared a relapse after the war. Jim Crow still lived in some areas, schools remained segregated, parts of the South resisted giving the franchise to Negroes, and treatment under the law was still unequal in some areas. The war years, however, certainly hastened postwar integration in the armed services and generally advanced civil rights.

All the changes introduced during World War II did not contribute to advances for the Negro. The activist March on Washington threatened the government, but it was an empty threat during the war years. World War II probably delayed concerted activism for many years. Millions of young Negroes in the armed services were frustrated, yet they adjusted to the regulated life because opportunities appeared better in the service. The armed services moved toward integration faster than civilian society, and the Korean War proved that integration provided the most effective use of military manpower. Yet, the armed services did little to train Negro leaders during World War II, and those who received commissions were sometimes baffled by their experiences. Most Negroes, however, accepted the rigors of wartime duty as a temporary state of affairs to be followed by a return to normal civilian life.

The war brought large numbers of Negroes and whites together, and there were instances of friction and violence. The riots during the summer of 1943 and the "harvest of disorders" within the armed services undoubtedly damaged race relations, but the war made many people realize that racism was morally wrong and an impediment to the war effort.

The animosities pent up during the war surfaced immediately following the conflict. Some individuals in the South who held back their racist feelings in wartime saw to it that the homecoming of Negro servicemen was less than a glorious occasion. Nonetheless, the war produced thousands of Negro veterans who returned home with a new concept of what life should be like.[2] Despite the temporary disorders, advances made were advances retained, even in the South.

---

[2] See, for example, Richard M. Dalfiume, *Desegregation of the Armed Forces: Fighting on Two Fronts, 1939–1953* (Columbia: University of Missouri Press, 1969), p. 132.

Selected Bibliography

Manuscript Collections

National Association for the Advancement of Colored People. Files in Manuscript Division of the Library of Congress. National Urban League. Files in Manuscript Division of the Library of Congress.

Books

BILLINGSLEY, ANDREW. *Black Families in White America*. Englewood Cliffs, N.J.: Prentice-Hall, 1968.

CANTOR, MILTON, ed. *Black Labor in America*. Westport, Conn.: Negro Universities Press, 1969.

CARR, ROBERT K. *Federal Protection of Civil Rights: Quest for a Sword*. Ithaca, N.Y.: Cornell University Press, 1947.

Chicago Commission on Race Relations. *The Negro in Chicago: A Study of Race Relations and a Race Riot*. Chicago: University of Chicago Press, 1922.

CONN, STETSON; ENGELMAN, ROSE C.; and FAIRCHILD, BYRON. *Guarding the United States and Its Outposts*. The United States Army in World War II: The Western Hemisphere. Washington, D.C.: U.S. Government Printing Office, 1964.

DALFIUME, RICHARD M. *Desegregation of the Armed Forces: Fighting on Two Fronts, 1939–1953*. Columbia: University of Missouri Press, 1969.

DAVIE, MAURICE R. *Negroes in American Society*. New York: Whittlesey House, 1949.

DAVIS, ALLISON, and DOLLARD, JOHN. *Children of Bondage: The Personality Development of Negro Youth in the Urban South*. Washington, D.C.: American Council on Education, 1940.

DAVIS, ALLISON; GARDNER, BURLEIGH B.; and GARDNER, MARY R. *Deep South*. Chicago: University of Chicago Press, 1941.

DOLLARD, JOHN. *Caste and Class in a Southern Town*. New Haven: Yale University Press, 1937.

DOYLE, BERTRAM WILBUR. *The Etiquette of Race Relations in the South: A Study in Social Control*. 1937. Port Washington, N.Y.: Kennikat Press, 1968.

DRAKE, ST. CLAIR, and CAYTON, HORACE R. *Black Metropolis: A Study of Negro Life in a Northern City.* New York: Harcourt, Brace, 1945.

✳ EISENHOWER, DWIGHT D. *The Papers of Dwight D. Eisenhower: The War Years.* Vol 4. Baltimore: Johns Hopkins Press, 1970.

FOGEL, WALTER A. *The Negro in the Meat Industry.* The Racial Policies of American Industry, Report No. 12. Philadelphia: University of Pennsylvania Press, 1970.

FRAZIER, E. FRANKLIN. *The Negro Family in the United States.* Chicago: University of Chicago Press, 1939.

———. *The Negro in the United States.* Rev. ed. New York: Macmillan, 1957.

GARFINKEL, HERBERT. *When Negroes March: The March on Washington Movement in the Organizational Politics for FEPC.* Glencoe, Ill.: Free Press, 1959.

GRIMSHAW, ALLEN D., ed. *Racial Violence in the United States.* Chicago: Aldine, 1969.

HARRIS, ABRAM L. *The Negro as Capitalist: A Study of Banking and Business Among American Negroes.* 1936. College Park, Md.: McGrath, 1968.

HOLT, RACKHAM. *Mary McLeod Bethune: A Biography.* Garden City, N.Y.: Doubleday, 1964.

JEFFRESS, PHILIP W. *The Negro in the Urban Transit Industry.* The Racial Policies of American Industry, Report No. 18. Philadelphia: University of Pennsylvania Press, 1970.

JOHNSON, CHARLES S. *Patterns of Negro Segregation.* New York: Harper & Brothers, 1943.

KAMMERER, GLADYS M. *Impact of War on Federal Personnel Administration 1939–1945.* Lexington: University of Kentucky Press, 1951.

KARIG, WALTER, and KELLEY, WELLBOURN. *Battle Report: Pearl Harbor to Coral Sea.* New York: Farrar & Rinehart, 1944.

KENNEDY, LOUISE VENABLE. *The Negro Peasant Turns Cityward.* 1930. New York: AMS Press, 1968.

KESSELMAN, LOUIS COLERIDGE. *The Social Politics of FEPC: A Study in Reform Pressure Movements.* Chapel Hill: University of North Carolina Press, 1948.

KEY, V. O., JR. *Southern Politics in State and Nation.* New York: Alfred A. Knopf, 1949.

KING, CARL B., and RISHER, HOWARD W., JR. *The Negro in the Petroleum Industry.* The Racial Policies of American Industry, Report No. 5. Philadelphia: University of Pennsylvania Press, 1969.

KRISLOV, SAMUEL. *The Negro in Federal Employment: The Quest for Equal Opportunity.* Minneapolis: University of Minnesota Press, 1967.

LEE, ALFRED McCLUNG, and HUMPHREY, NORMAN DAYMOND. *Race Riot.* New York: Dryden Press, 1943.

LEE, ULYSSES. *The Employment of Negro Troops.* The United States Army in World War II: Special Studies. Washington, D.C.: U.S. Government Printing Office, 1966.

LOGAN, RAYFORD W., ed. *What the Negro Wants.* Chapel Hill: University of North Carolina Press, 1944.

MOON, BUCKLIN. *Primer for White Folks.* New York: Doubleday, Doran, 1945.

MYRDAL, GUNNAR. *An American Dilemma: The Negro Problem and Modern Democracy.* New York: Harper & Row, 1962.

NELSON, DENNIS D. *The Integration of the Negro into the U.S. Navy.* New York: Farrar, Straus & Young, 1951.

NORTHRUP, HERBERT R. *The Negro in the Aerospace Industry.* The Racial Policies of American Industry, Report No. 2. Philadelphia: University of Pennsylvania Press, 1968.

————. *The Negro in the Automobile Industry.* The Racial Policies of American Industry, Report No. 1. Philadelphia: University of Pennsylvania Press, 1968.

————. *The Negro in the Rubber Tire Industry.* The Racial Policies of American Industry, Report No. 6. Philadelphia: University of Pennsylvania Press, 1969.

————. *Organized Labor and the Negro.* New York: Harper & Brothers, 1944.

OTTLEY, ROI. *Inside Black America.* London: Eyre & Spottiswoode, 1948.

PALMER, ROBERT R.; WILEY, BELL I.; and KEAST, WILLIAM R. *The Procurement and Training of Ground Combat Troops.* The United States Army in World War II: The Army Ground Forces. Washington, D.C.: U.S. Government Printing Office, 1948.

POWDERMAKER, HORTENSE. *After Freedom: A Cultural History of the Deep South.* New York: Viking Press, 1939.

RECORD, WILSON. *The Negro and the Communist Party.* Chapel Hill: University of North Carolina Press, 1951.

ROOSEVELT, FRANKLIN D. *Public Papers and Addresses of Franklin D. Roosevelt.* New York: Random House, 1950.

Ross, Malcolm. *All Manner of Men.* New York: Greenwood Press, 1948.

Rowan, Richard L. *The Negro in the Steel Industry.* The Racial Policies of American Industry, Report No. 3. Philadelphia: University of Pennsylvania Press, 1968.

Ruchames, Louis. *Race, Jobs, & Politics: The Story of FEPC.* New York: Columbia University Press, 1953.

Ruppenthal, Roland G. *Logistical Support of the Armies.* The United States Army in World War II: The European Theater of Operations. Washington, D.C.: Office of the Chief of Military History, Department of the Army, 1959.

Shogan, Robert, and Craig, Tom. *The Detroit Race Riot: A Study in Violence.* Philadelphia: Chilton Books, 1964.

Smith, Clarence McKittrick. *The Medical Department: Hospitalization and Evacuation, Zone of Interior.* The United States Army in World War II: The Technical Services. Washington, D.C.: Office of the Chief of Military History, Department of the Army, 1956.

Spero, Sterling D., and Harris, Abram L. *The Black Worker: The Negro and the Labor Movement.* 1931. Port Washington, N.Y.: Kennikat Press, 1966.

St. James, Warren D. *The National Association for the Advancement of Colored People: A Case Study in Pressure Groups.* New York: Exposition Press, 1958.

Sterner, Richard. *The Negro's Share: A Study of Income, Consumption, Housing and Public Assistance.* New York: Harper & Brothers, 1943.

Sutherland, Robert L. *Color, Class, and Personality.* Washington, D.C.: American Council on Education, 1942.

Treadwell, Mattie E. *The Women's Army Corps.* The United States Army in World War II: Special Studies. Washington, D.C.: Office of the Chief of Military History, Department of the Army, 1954.

U.S. Office of Education. *National Survey of the Higher Education of Negroes.* Vol. 4, *A Summary,* by Ambrose Caliver. Washington, D.C.: U.S. Government Printing Office, 1943.

Van Riper, Paul P. *History of the United States Civil Service.* Evanston: Row, Peterson, 1958.

Weaver, Robert C. *The Negro Ghetto.* New York: Harcourt, Brace, 1948.

———. *Negro Labor: A National Problem.* New York: Harcourt, Brace, 1946.

WHITE, WALTER. *A Man Called White: The Autobiography of Walter White.* New York: Viking Press, 1948.

———. *A Rising Wind.* New York: Doubleday, Doran, 1945.

WOLTERS, RAYMOND. *Negroes and the Great Depression: The Problem of Economic Recovery.* Westport, Conn.: Greenwood, 1970.

Articles

ANDERSON, MARY. "Negro Women on the Production Front." *Opportunity* 21 (April 1943): 37–38.

BERKLEY, CHARLES C. "War Work—A Challenge to Negro Womanpower." *Opportunity* 21 (April 1943): 58–59.

BETHUNE, MARY McLEOD. "My Secret Talks with FDR." *Ebony* (April 1949): 42–51.

BROWN, EARL. "American Negroes and the War." *Harper's Magazine* (April 1942): 545–52.

———. "The Truth about the Detroit Riot." *Harper's Magazine* (November 1943): 488–98.

DeMAR, GEORGE E. "Negro Women Are American Workers, Too." *Opportunity* 21 (April 1943): 41.

DuBois, W. E. B. "Documents of the War." *Crisis* 18 (May 1919): 16–21.

GLOSTER, HUGH M. "Richard Wright: Interpreter of Racial and Economic Maladjustments." *Opportunity* 19 (December 1941): 361.

GRANGER, LESTER B. "The President, the Negro, and Defense." *Opportunity* 19 (July 1941): 204.

———. "Victory Through Unity." *Opportunity* 21 (October 1943): 147–51.

HIMES, CHESTER B. "Zoot Riots Are Race Riots." *Crisis* 50 (July 1943): 200.

JEFFRIES, LeROY W. "Step Up, Lady—Want a War Job?" *Opportunity* 21 (April 1943): 39.

JOHNSON, CHARLES S. "The Negro Minority." *Annals of the American Academy of Political and Social Science* 223 (September 1942): 10–16.

JULIAN-BROWN, MATTIE. "Train Today for Today's Jobs!" *Opportunity* 20 (May 1942): 138–39.

KONVITZ, MILTON R. "A Nation Within a Nation: The Negro and the Supreme Court." *Opportunity* 20 (June 1942): 175.

LAUTIER, LOUIS. "Sidelights on the Negro and the Army." *Opportunity* 22 (January–March 1944): 5.

LEWIS, ALFRED BAKER. "Reducing Racial Tensions." *Opportunity* 21 (October 1943): 156.

MARSHALL, THURGOOD. "The Gestapo in Detroit." *Crisis* 50 (August 1943): 232.

————. "Negro Status in the Boilermakers Union." *Crisis* 51 (March 1944): 77–78.

MURRAY, PAULI. "A Blueprint for First Class Citizenship." *Crisis* 51 (November 1944): 358–59.

PECK, JAMES L. H. "When Do *We* Fly?" *Crisis* 47 (December 1940): 376.

REDDICK, LAWRENCE D. "The Negro in the United States Navy During World War II." *Journal of Negro History* 32 (April 1947): 201–19.

RIDDLE, ESTELLE MASSEY. "The Negro Nurse and the War." *Opportunity* 21 (April 1943): 44.

THOMAS, JULIUS A. "Race Conflict and Social Action." *Opportunity* 21 (October 1943): 165.

"White Policemen in Harlem." *Crisis* 52 (January 1945): 16–17.

WILKINS, ROY. "Nurses Go to War." *Crisis* 50 (February 1943): 42–44.

YOUNG, P. B. "The Negro Press—Today and Tomorrow." *Opportunity* 17 (July 1939): 204–05.

Index

Black Americans in World War II, by A. Russell Buchanan, was copy edited by Paulette Wamego, proofread by Barbara Phillips, and designed by Lloyd W. Garrison and Shelly Lowenkopf. The cover design was executed by Jack Swartz. Composition in linotype Baskerville was done by Kimberly Press, Goleta, Calif. Printing was also done by Kimberly Press.